VIETNAM VIGNETTES

To Weldon —
With deep appreciation for
Your service to our nation

Hanoi •

•**Haiphong**

Gulf of Tonkin

•Quang Tri
Hue• •

•Da Nang

Chu Lai

•Quang Ngai

VIETNAM

•**Pleiku** •**Qui Nhon**

Tuy Hoa•

•Ban Me Thuot

Nha Trang•

Cam Ranh Bay•

*South
China
Sea*

•Tay Ninh

Saigon • •**Bien Hoa**

My Tho• •Vung Tau

•Can Tho

VIETNAM VIGNETTES

Tales of an Infantryman

LEE BASNAR

Printed in 2004.
Printed in the United States of America.
ISBN 1-59113-512-5
Published by Booklocker.com, Inc.
www.booklocker.com

Front cover photos
Left: The author, center, interrogates a captured Viet Cong soldier in Binh Dinh province. August 1967.
Center: In Quang Ngai province, a platoon medic bandages jungle rot on a soldier's legs while another soldier reads a letter from home. November 1970.
Right: A Vietnamese peasant weaves a basket from split bamboo near the village of Tra Binh. January 1971.

Back cover photo
Self-portrait of Lee Basnar. April 2004.

Cover and interior photos are from the Lee Basnar collection.

Vietnam map adapted from
http://www.lib.utexas.edu/maps/middle_east_and_asia/vietnam_pol92.jpg

Cover design and interior design by Lorraine B. Elder.

To the Officers and Men of C Company
1st Battalion, 52nd Infantry
198th Infantry Brigade
Americal Division

You fought hard,
suffered much,
and bear the scars,
both visible and invisible.
May your remaining years
be filled with the satisfaction
that you did your job well,
and may you never forget
our absent comrades.

Foreword

Each generation of Americans since this country was founded has called on its young men to make sacrifices on the battlefield. Each generation has transformed young men from ordinary citizens into warriors who performed deeds not imaginable by the average person. These young warriors came home and were expected to blend back into society as if they had never left, their experiences locked up, only to be released on special occasions.

Each war has produced a few good books describing life in the trenches, but usually they focus on a few individuals or special units, ignoring the true heroes: the infantrymen, or "grunts." *Vietnam Vignettes* is one of those rare works that show life as it was for those in conventional units, slugging it out with the enemy and living daily life between battles. Each deadly encounter in *Vietnam Vignettes* accurately depicts the excitement and danger of combat and the sacrifices the grunts made for their buddies. It describes the routine of the battlefield, and the awesome responsibility of command to keep the soldiers on their toes.

The author has a special talent for giving the reader the view from both the officer's and the enlisted man's side. While no individuals are singled out by name for doing great deeds or for being not-so-great officers, the author skillfully describes situations that affected the life of the grunt. To use names would take away from the true value of the book and from the credit due the common infantryman.

Vietnam Vignettes recognizes our true heroes, gives family members a better understanding of what their loved ones went through, and what may have been going on in their minds while they were away.

Those of us who had the great honor of leading our fine young soldiers in battle know how special this generation is. The Vietnam War was our nation's longest war, and I suggest that it rivals the American Civil War for dividing the nation. The draftees and enlistees went to Vietnam despite having many reasons to justify not going. Politicians, clergy, educators and even movie stars were protesting the war, and yet most soldiers went into danger because of a sense of duty or honor.

Most combat commanders know who the real heroes are and will applaud this book that honors them. Thank you, Lee Basnar, for your service to your country, and thank you for *Vietnam Vignettes!*

Drew Dix

MAJOR
U.S. ARMY (RETIRED)
MEDAL OF HONOR RECIPIENT

CONTENTS

PART III   ON THE WAY. WAIT.

Preface

...His vision dims, and yesteryear
Is vividly revealed.
He hears the cannon, fights the fear
In far-off battlefields...

Excerpt from the poem
"A Soldier Retires"
by Lee Basnar

This book describes what it was like to be an infantryman fighting on Vietnam's coastal plain and in the jungles in the area known as II Corps and I Corps. The years described include 1967–1968 and 1970–1971. Those are the years I served in that war, and the men whose actions I describe are either South Vietnamese soldiers whom I advised during my first tour, or American soldiers whom I led during my second tour.

Infantrymen in all wars share common experiences, and every grunt who fought in Vietnam will recognize scenes and descriptions in this book that he'll swear happened in his unit or in the one next to his.

In one instance, using creative nonfiction, I compiled memories of individuals' dialogue and several battle scenes into one chapter, "Keep Your Head Down," rather than scatter the scenes throughout the book.

There was no other way to depict the bonding of infantrymen under fire. Otherwise, the tales in this book show the action and incidents as I remember them.

Every infantryman retains memories of firefights, booby traps, mines, and spider holes. Two soldiers who fought side by side in the same battle will remember and describe the action differently. Each infantry unit developed a distinct personality, and each tour, for those who spent more than one tour over there, was a unique experience.

Vietnam affected a generation of Americans, as did World Wars I and II and the Korean War. Although not global in scale like the world wars, nor fought in set-piece battles over key terrain like the Korean War, the Vietnam War lasted longer than the United States' involvement in the other three wars combined. Tens of thousands of Americans died in Vietnam, and hundreds of thousands suffered injuries from wounds, accidents, and mental trauma.

This book is not about the scale of the war nor about American casualty statistics and enemy body counts. It's not about high-level tactics and large battles. It's not about strategic objectives, nor about the political ramifications of fighting and eventually giving up on the war. These are my memories of the beauty and the ugliness of South Vietnam, of the monsoons, the odors, the rattle of machine guns, the tracers lashing the darkness, the misery and the humor, and the tough life of an infantryman in Charlie Company.

Lee Basnar

SIERRA VISTA, ARIZONA
2004

SFC Lee Basnar at Ba Gi.
March 1968

Part I

Opening the Duffel Bag

Chapter 1

Images of Vietnam

W hen I recall the years when I fought in Vietnam, images flash at random. Some are as sharp as a bayonet; others, dulled by the passage of time, are stuffed into the bottom of my mental duffel bag. I open that duffel bag now and peer cautiously into that memory hoard, reluctant to examine too closely the painful scenes that rise from the dust and mud of bygone battles. Images slowly come into focus through the haze of passing years.

Tropical heat, wavering above asphalt runways and crowded city streets, distorted distant objects the way rippling water alters the shape of submerged stones. Aboard an olive drab army bus that plowed through those shimmering waves, I gazed out open windows covered by stout mesh. The wire prevented shapely young ladies on bicycles, and button-nosed children, from tossing hand grenades into the busload of arriving soldiers.

The bus crept along Saigon's cluttered streets, inching forward among pedicabs, cyclos (three-wheeled, motorized taxis), motorbikes, and rattletrap blue-and-yellow Renault taxis. The red-orange sun was disappearing, and dusk made faster progress through the city than we did.

A blue-gray haze enveloped us, stinking of partially combusted fuel from hordes of ancient, inefficient engines. The burnt-alcohol odor of exhaust from Lambrettas and motorbikes hung in the air, a gray and dirty scent. Obnoxious diesel exhaust blackened the air when American military trucks passed. The exhaust from gridlocked traffic formed a polluted cloud. Soon fires flickered in the braziers of sidewalk vendors, adding more smoke to the haze that smothered Saigon.

I was reminded of Juarez, Mexico, a city that crowded the international border next to El Paso, Texas. While I studied Vietnamese at the Defense Language Institute at Fort Bliss, adjacent to El Paso, my wife and I occasionally walked across the footbridge into Ciudad Juarez. Poverty ignores international boundaries; street scenes in Mexico resembled those outside our bus in Saigon.

I studied the men seated near me in the bus. We were all slated to become advisors, and we were, for the most part, career noncommissioned officers, although a few draftees and specialists clustered at the rear of the bus. Only three of the soldiers looked older than thirty, and most were in their early-to-mid twenties. Two sergeants were "old Asia hands," a term for soldiers who'd already served one or more tours in Southeast Asia. The rest of us were "cherries," soldiers beginning our first tour in a combat zone. We seldom spoke, preferring to stare at the teeming city that hindered our passage. Cigarette smoke floated out through the open bus windows, adding a minor contribution to the foul air outside.

We arrived at the Military Assistance Command, Vietnam (MACV) processing center, where soldiers destined to become advisors received their initial orientation. Its name was Koelper Compound, an appropriated hotel renamed for Marine Captain Donald E. Koelper, the first U.S. Marine to die in the Vietnam War. The Navy Cross recipient was killed in action three years before I arrived in Vietnam in 1967.

Sandbags piled head-high formed a circular guard post next to a gate that swung open when we reached it, and two military policemen waved the bus into the former courtyard, which had been transformed into an assembly area where we would gather prior to attending classes in the hotel annex.

Aside from the concrete-block wall and triple concertina wire that surrounded the building, the exterior of the hotel reminded me of hotels I saw during an earlier tour of duty in France. The design was French, and a dull yellowish-beige paint covered the stucco, which had flaked off these walls in several places, afflicting the building with tropical acne.

Resemblance to the French hospitality industry ended when I entered the old hotel. Concrete blocks plugged holes where ground-floor windows once looked onto the street, and the upstairs reeked from the suffocating stench of blocked toilets. Water trickled periodically through ancient pipes, but toilet users couldn't wait until the next surge of intermittent electricity powered the water pumps. Piles of feces filled the commodes; when the water did flow, the excrement plugged the sewer pipes, forcing sewage out onto the broken tiles that freckled the concrete floor. Old Vietnamese women, their teeth stained black from chewing betel nut, languidly cleaned up the mess. Occasionally, using broken English, they joked with the new arrivals. I couldn't imagine the poverty that would make a person seek such a job.

Sweat-drenched in the heat and humidity, I tossed my duffel bag onto one of four bunks in a tiny room. Because of the late hour, we'd begin our orientation tomorrow. I decided to walk across the street to another U.S. Army-appropriated hotel that served as a mess hall, lounge, and administration center. Thirsty and tired from the twenty-two-hour flight across the Pacific Ocean, which included stops at Hawaii, Wake Island, and Japan, I was eager to drink a cold beer. When I stepped into the street, kids dashed up to me, shouting, "Number one! OK! OK! Hallo! Hallo!" They swarmed around me, grabbed my hands, tried to lift my wallet from my hip pocket, and nearly tore my watch from my wrist. I told them, in their language, to behave or I'd call the police. Although they were surprised to hear me speak Vietnamese, they laughed at the idea of the police paying any attention to their attempted thievery.

Along the city sidewalks, piles of garbage fouled the air with the stench of rotten fruit, decomposing fish, human feces, urine, and unidentified repulsive odors. Next to a pile of refuse, charcoal braziers added their burnt-wood smell to the tantalizing scent of cooked shrimp and soy sauce. Prostitutes ambled along the sidewalks, surrounded by an invisible cloud of cheap perfume.

The sidewalks around the military compound teemed with merchants trying to sell me watches, beer, drugs, love beads, U.S. Army fatigues, crude maps of Vietnam made from flattened beer cans, rice, chicken, fish, and even loaves of French bread. Still under assault from the kids, I was uneasy about being alone and without a weapon. Although I figured the Viet Cong (VC) wouldn't risk shooting me in such a crowded place, I was eager to cross the busy street to the safety of the concrete hotel.

I shook loose from the street beggars, weaved through a stream of cyclos that swerved toward me as their drivers demanded that I ride with them, nodded and grinned at the MPs who guarded the entrance, and entered the lobby of the five-story hotel. I took a deep breath and realized I didn't smell the odor of plugged plumbing. I concluded that perhaps officers stayed in this building. I rode the elevator to the rooftop open-air restaurant, where I ordered a beer and a steak from a tiny Vietnamese waitress who spoke a little English. Her crooked teeth detracted from her broad smile, and she wore oversized U.S. Army cook's whites, a shapeless covering that discouraged GIs from staring at her body. The sun had dropped behind the building-cluttered horizon a long time ago, but the temperature must have been in the high nineties. I wondered if I'd ever be cool and dry again. Another sergeant joined me, and we exchanged the usual soldier chatter. We discussed hometowns, time in service, last duty assignment, military occupational specialty (MOS), and other trivia, but we didn't mention how we felt about spending our first night in Vietnam, or facing 364 nights in this country before we could return home.

The waitress served me a Carlings Black Label beer, leathery steak, and limp french fries and trotted away, her flip-flops slapping against her heels. The sergeant had eaten, so he headed for the bar while I sawed away at the steak and poured ketchup on the greasy fries.

I watched red tracers stream down through the darkness a few kilometers to the north. No noise, no sense of danger, only the tracers. A white flare erupted amid the tracers and floated toward the earth, displacing the darkness, dimming as it disappeared behind who-knows-what, quickly replaced by another flare, and then another. The distant crump of an exploding artillery shell reached my ears, but the roar of two- and four-cycle engines, the constant beeping of horns, and the occasional blast of a policeman's whistle in the street five stories below me overwhelmed most sounds of the far-off combat. I tried to imagine the action taking place beneath those flares. Were men suffering, dying? How would I react when I faced combat? No longer hungry, I ignored my steak, now cold and unappealing. I finished my beer and left, returning to the processing center.

I was eager to finish processing and report to my unit, wherever that was. The daily classes bored me. Inept instructors who spoke little Vietnamese attempted to teach us a few phrases. Other sergeants offered an overview of Vietnam's history and some of the Vietnamese customs and traditions, but I had spent the previous nine months learning those subjects in detail. Other instructors explained our role as advisors, which did interest me, but I struggled to stay awake in the hot and humid classroom.

Finally, after one week, processing ended and I received my assignment. I learned that—because I was an infantry noncommissioned officer (NCO) who was school-trained in the Vietnamese language—I would serve as an advisor in the Army of the Republic of Vietnam's (ARVN) 22nd Infantry Division. The division was headquartered in Qui Nhon, a port on the South China Sea roughly halfway between Saigon and the demilitarized zone (DMZ) that divided the two Vietnams.

I headed north to join MACV Team 22, flying in a C-130 Hercules over miles of bright green rice paddies. I wondered about the lives of the Vietnamese people far below me. The plane banked sharply, taking up a new heading, vectoring around jets swooping to drop bombs in support of friendly troops. Smoke rose from jungled hills, but from our height I detected little ground activity.

At Pleiku, I wandered outside the airfield terminal to stretch my legs during an intermediate stop and saw the effects of heavy combat. A recent battle for some unknown hill had resulted in many American casualties; six battle-weary veterans of that fight sat on their packs, sweating in the sun. I noted their torn and filthy jungle fatigues, matted and mud-caked hair, and grimy faces covered with whisker stubble.

But their eyes told the story, old eyes in young warriors, aged by indescribable experiences. The soldiers gazed my way, but they looked through me, not at me, staring at some scene from hell, visible only to them. They ignored one another, waiting for some unwelcome event, perhaps a helicopter ride to another location where they would again face the enemy. I studied their faces, but saw no hope in their expressions. Exhaustion, resignation, despair, but not hope. Would I look like that in the coming months?

North of Qui Nhon, the South China Sea splashed gently onto deserted beaches and sent needles of reflected sunlight through my jeep's windshield. For miles and miles, a narrow strip of barren sand separated dense vegetation from the restless water. Interrupted occasionally by trunks of coconut palms or outcroppings of black, jagged rocks, the beaches evoked images of the Pacific Islands of World War II. Fish, lobsters, and huge prawns thrived in the warm waters, and Vietnamese fishermen reaped the plenitude, bobbing about in their little round basket boats like rafters bouncing through rapids. Directional control must have been difficult, but the fishermen maneuvered skillfully in spite of wind, tide, and current.

Highway 1 paralleled the seacoast. A potholed, spine-jarring, asphalt-and-dirt roadway, the country's unreliable main highway led from the south, near Saigon, to the DMZ and beyond in the north. Closed often because of enemy activity, with no original bridges remaining to span the many rivers, the road appeared deceptively peaceful under the midday sun as it sliced between rice fields and wound through mountain passes. At night no one ventured far on Highway 1—the Street Without Joy.

The VC controlled the highway at night, blowing up temporary bridges or detonating mines beneath those foolish enough to challenge the enemy's dominion between dusk and dawn. In northern Binh Dinh Province, the VC blew the Bong Son Bridge several times, as well as the temporary bridge constructed to replace it. Enemy snipers harassed the South Vietnamese Popular Force (PF) soldiers who guarded the bridge. When the enemy attacked in force, the PF troops withdrew into the night, preferring to run rather than confront Viet Cong administered torture and death. Neither the leaders nor their soldiers had much training, and both were reluctant to fight the VC, some of whom were from the same villages as the PF soldiers.

Water wheel irrigates crops in An Lao Valley.
July 1967

Not far from the Bong Son Bridge, two teenage Vietnamese girls irrigated a rice paddy. Their equipment consisted of two ropes attached to opposing sides of a conical basket. When they relaxed their tension on the ropes, the basket descended into a shallow well and filled with water. Then, opposite each other, they pulled on the ropes, causing the ropes to tighten and the basket to rise. With an easy rhythm, they swung the basket over an adjacent dike, spilling water into a shallow canal that led to nearby rice fields. They spent endless hours under the hot sun, pulling, tossing, relaxing, repeating. Food production placed heavy labor demands on the peasants. Later, the VC would demand a portion of the harvest as taxes, and the South Vietnamese government would claim its share too. American troops searching villages for enemy rice caches would bag and ship tons of the confiscated grain to so-called pacified villages. The girls' work at the irrigation well began a chain of events that, like so many events in that war, led in directions few could anticipate.

Other women trotted along trails and dusty roads, with long bamboo poles on their shoulders bearing the weight of water pails, or perhaps baskets of mangoes or breadfruit. The baskets, suspended from the ends of the poles, counterbalanced each other, stabilizing the load. The women developed a hip-swinging gait that allowed them to cover ground quickly yet not cause the baskets or pails at the ends of the poles to bob and sway. Bare feet slap-slapped on the packed trail as the women passed. Conical coolie hats shielded their faces, and long-sleeved black pajamas protected their bodies from the blazing sun. Unlike GIs, the Vietnamese didn't deliberately expose their skin to the sun.

Chapter 2

Tet, 1968

The ARVN 22nd Infantry Division headquarters moved from Qui Nhon, where I had joined the advisory team six months before, to the tiny village of Ba Gi, an hour's drive northwest on Highway 1. Near the junction of Highway 1 and Highway 19, crumbling monuments from the Cham dynasty, which ruled the country from the second to the twelfth centuries, cast morning shadows over the collection of crude huts that served as home to the dependents of the soldiers who served at the headquarters.

Triple concertina wire stitched widely separated guard towers together and surrounded the headquarters compound, which included a white headquarters building with a corrugated steel roof, and smaller, slap-dash structures where operations, administrative and supply officers worked. Advisors occupied a corner of the twelve-acre compound, and enjoyed the luxury of tropical-style, open-sided screened buildings that resisted the ubiquitous mosquitoes. A mess hall and small club provided reasonably edible food and cold American beer.

ARVN 22d Infantry Division Headquarters at Ba Gi.
March 1968

View from Monument Hill at Ba Gi.
February 1968

One of the Vietnamese officers whom I advised invited me to Tet dinner in his hut. Nghia was a *chuan uy,* or aspirant, similar to perhaps a third lieutenant, if such a grade had actually existed in our army. If he proved himself worthy, and maybe greased enough palms, his superiors would promote the aspirant to second lieutenant.

Chuan Uy Nghia and his lovely wife were excellent hosts under the circumstances. When I arrived at their home after the half-mile walk from the division headquarters, they greeted me and said, *"Chuc Trung Si may man,"* which loosely translated to "We wish you much luck, Sergeant." It was one way of saying "Happy New Year." *"Chuc Mung Nam Moi"* was another. Nghia introduced me to his wife, who looked lovely and festive in her *ao dai* of white silk embroidered with red and gold flowers. The ao dai was sort of a one-piece shirt and over-skirt worn over, in this case, white silk slacks. The skirt portion, split from the ankles nearly to the waist, fell gracefully over the slacks in front and back.

Their home, a battered plywood hut perched on stilts over a slough that lapped against rice paddy dikes, consisted of two tiny rooms and an attached outdoor platform that served as a combination toilet and kitchen. There was practically no furniture. Nghia's wife prepared meals while squatting on the floor next to charcoal braziers where she cooked the food. Battered 5-gallon cans held water for cooking and dish washing.

The main room served as a dining room, living room, and shrine to departed ancestors. Tan straw floor mats surrounded an 18-inch-high battered table. Smaller woven-grass place mats covered the scarred tabletop. In one corner, incense smoke twisted in the faint breeze that drifted through the wall openings that served in place of windows. A vase of flowers, some photos, and a couple of paintings of loved ones, apparently dead ancestors, composed the shrine's centerpiece. The other room served as a bedroom for the Nghias and their two small children.

Ba Gi village near 22d ARVN Infantry Division Headquarters.
April 1968

The Vietnamese I served with and advised seldom drank alcohol, or, if they did, not much. Maybe that was because their beer tasted so bad. If the local beer had been my only option I would have become a teetotaler. Vietnamese beer, *Ba Muoi Ba* (Thirty-Three), smelled like formaldehyde and tasted like it smelled. GIs referred to the beer as "Bomb-t-Bomb." Biere Larue, a French beer, was nearly as bad. It smelled like old, sweaty GI socks, and the taste matched the odor.

The Vietnamese knew that Americans liked to drink booze, and on this occasion my hosts treated me to what they thought was American hospitality and a combination of an American New Year and a Vietnamese Tet celebration. I barely had time to hand my gifts to Nghia before he handed me a glass full of Scotch. No ice, no soda, no water, just Scotch. I sipped, shuddered, and smiled to show how much I appreciated his gesture. Nghia beamed. The hostess giggled, smiled, clamped her hand over her mouth, and looked down at the rough floor to avoid eye contact with me. She promptly disappeared onto the outdoor balcony and resumed dinner preparations.

Nghia spoke almost no English, but we conversed quite well in Vietnamese. We discussed the United States, but I had to describe any place I mentioned in terms of how far it was from *Nu U'uoc* (New York), which was about the only American city he'd heard of.

We also talked about recent battles and our hopes for the new year, and I explained our New Year's Eve traditions as well as I could in his language. I complimented him on his home. As humble as it was, its salvaged plywood walls and recycled corrugated metal roof were upscale for such a low-ranking officer. Nghia reached over and held my hand in a gesture of friendship, but that action, natural to Vietnamese males, made me uncomfortable. He urged me to drink the Scotch, apparently not realizing that if I drank that much alcohol in a hurry I'd be knee-walking drunk in short order.

Eventually, his wife served the meal prepared especially for me, for I was the guest of honor. Although I had eaten Vietnamese food for six months by now and was accustomed to it, Nghia surprised me with one of the courses. The centerpiece, or main course, was a fish that looked like a carp. I don't know the proper name of the fish, but we Americans called them bamboo trout. Nghia reached over, took my bowl, stabbed into the bamboo trout with his chopsticks, laid some fish portions into my bowl, and then extracted the stomach from the cooked fish. With a flourish, he placed the stomach into my wooden bowl and presented it to me. Not satisfied, he then plucked one eyeball from the fish and added that to the bowl.

I gladly gulped more Scotch when I realized I would have to eat that damned stomach, which contained what appeared to be bugs, beetles, and other water insects. To refuse would have insulted my host and hostess, which was unthinkable. The eyeball went down easily, but trying to manipulate that stomach with chopsticks and bite off a small piece without dropping the entire mess onto the table, well, I couldn't master that. I dropped the stomach back into the bowl and asked my host where the bathroom was. He directed me to the balcony, the same place where his wife squatted on the floor and labored over the next course. Nghia pointed to the slough below and told me that was the bathroom. I faced the rail in full view of his wife, who graciously moved so her back was toward me, and as I peed into the slough I began to wonder if the carp was caught right there, in the pool that served as an outhouse. Quite likely, I thought.

The stomach awaited me at the table, but I now had a plan. I'd drink more Scotch, fake having to pee again, and deposit that damned stomach into the slough on my next trip to the balcony. I picked away at some of the meat that still remained on the fish carcass, and resisted my host's encouragement to swallow that stomach. He kept my glass brimful with Scotch, and I finally excused myself again, popped the stomach into my mouth, walked to the balcony, and spit the stomach over the railing into the darkness. My gustatory senses goaded me to vomit. I resisted the urge.

The meal consisted of other dishes, too, including beef cooked six different ways, a delicious Vietnamese specialty called *thit bo sau.* Nghia's wife brought and removed other dishes, but the Scotch fog I floated in dims my memory of them. I remember *thit ga* (chicken); *thit heo* (pork); and a dish that looked like pieces of stringy rat cooked in a stew. Nghia urged me to add *nuoc mam,* which was a fish sauce, to some of the dishes.

To make the tangy nuoc mam condiment, the Vietnamese alternated layers of stones with tiers of fish, five to seven levels high inside a large barrel. They added a few spices to each layer. As the fish rotted under the tropical sun, the resulting fluid filtered down through the strata. A simple faucet inserted at the bottom offered an exit for the foul-smelling mixture, which ended up in bottles. Few Vietnamese sat down to a meal without reaching for a nuoc mam bottle with which to flavor their food, similar to the way many Americans add ketchup or salsa to their meals.

Nghia continued to pour more Scotch. Because we sat around the table on floor mats, at least I avoided the danger of falling out of a chair from the effects of the booze. Rising without staggering was another matter, but I managed to get to my feet in a reasonably dignified fashion. At least I think I did.

With a belly full of Scotch, noodles, nuoc mam, fish, beef, pork, chicken, and who knows what else, I bid my hosts a happy Tet, wobbled across the catwalk to the bank, and stumbled through the darkness toward the advisors' compound. When out of the Nghias' hearing, I stopped, bent over from the waist, stuck my forefinger down my throat, and lightened my load.

A few hours later, mortar rounds and rocket-propelled grenades slammed into our perimeter, and the battle of Tet, 1968, began.

I remember that critical, nationwide battle well, but journalists and authors have used barrels of ink describing it in detail. When I recall Tet and the famous battle that lasted for days, I first think of peeing from the kitchen balcony while spitting a portion of a huge fish stomach into the slough below. It was a New Year's celebration to remember, or perhaps forget.

After I'd been in the country for more than seven months, it was my turn to take a three-day in-country rest-and-recreation leave (R&R), away from the stress of advising Vietnamese soldiers how to fight the war.

At the village of Vung Tau, which fronted on the South China Sea not far from Saigon, American soldiers sunbathed on a white-sand beach. We went to this in-country R&R site for one three-day period to relax and rest, enjoying a brief interlude from the demands and dangers of our jobs. Clerks and cooks, infantrymen and truck drivers, airmen, sailors, and marines shared a break at Vung Tau. We swam in the sea, drank cold beer, or just relaxed. The three days, however, was a myth—at least for me. I arrived at Vung Tau at 1800, or 6:00 p.m., which counted as day number one. I had to depart at 0800, or 8:00 a.m., on day number three. I spent one full day there, but as far as the army was concerned I had been there for three days.

I was an infantry sergeant during my first tour, and an infantry captain during my second. I compartmentalize those disparate recollections, as if I were two different individuals fighting in the same war at different times. Although I remember some of the Vietnamese officers such as Dai Uy (Captain) Hai, Chuan Uy Nghia, and Thieu Ta (Major) Tieu, among others, and some of my fellow American NCOs and officers, I push my first tour into the bottom of the memory duffel bag, where it's overwhelmed by the experience of commanding an American infantry company during my second tour. That tour now rises to the top of the duffel bag.

Shrine to ancestors in Tuy Hoa valley.
May 1968

PART II

COMMANDING CHARLIE COMPANY

Captain Lee C. Basnar, Charlie Company Commander
1970–1971

Chapter 3

Death by Monsoon

After the chartered passenger jet came to a stop at Bien Hoa Air Base, a blast of tropical heat rushed into the airplane through the open exit door. Riding the heat waves, unseen but pervasive, the odors of kerosene, hot asphalt, and the stink of diesel mixed with human feces—burning in the distance but contaminating the breeze—greeted us. This country still smelled just as bad as it did during my first tour.

My second tour in Vietnam started shortly before a storm roared ashore from the South China Sea. The flood forced me to wait an extra day at battalion headquarters in Chu Lai before boarding a chopper for LZ (landing zone) Stinson, where I would assume command of an infantry company: Charlie Company, 1st Battalion, 52d Infantry, 198th Infantry Brigade.

In the late summer of 1970, U.S. armed forces, experimenting with weather modification, salted clouds with chemicals in an attempt to create floods in North Vietnam. Unfortunately, the intensified storms lashed friendly troops in South Vietnam as well.

Twenty-nine inches of rain fell between September 29 and October 2, and all Americal Division units, including Charlie Company, suffered under the deluge.

After a low flight in reduced visibility over what looked like a lake dotted with grass shacks, trees, and hilltop islands poking up through brown, swirling waters that rushed across the coastal plain toward the sea, I arrived at the firebase. Firebases, also called LZs, supported infantry units with artillery and heavy mortar fire. Normally located on hills, the bases offered a vantage point from which to observe enemy ground movement across the adjacent plains.

LZ Stinson, occupying a hill now surrounded by submerged paddies and hedgerows, resembled an island in a huge, mud-stained lake. After we landed, I hoisted my duffel bag onto my shoulder, grabbed my M-16 rifle, and slogged through rain and mud up the hill to the battalion commander's bunker, where I reported to him. Inside the bunker, rain-soaked sandbags exuded the aroma of earth and mildew, joined by the oily odor of black tar applied to the bags to extend their useful life. A couple of light bulbs at the end of cords hung from the roof. The commander briefed me on my company's widely scattered locations, and then informed me that one of my platoons hadn't been heard from for more than twenty-four hours.

After the briefing, I realized I couldn't immediately join my dispersed company because of the lingering storm and approaching darkness. I made several attempts to contact the missing platoon by radio, with no luck.

The following morning, two members of the missing platoon, barefoot, limping, and without weapons or equipment, slogged onto LZ Stinson. One of the pair, the platoon sergeant, wore only an olive-drab nylon sleeping shirt and jungle-fatigue trousers rolled up to his knees.

The sergeant, whom the acting company commander had appointed as acting platoon leader, told me the story. They had established an NDP (night defensive position) and placed their MAs (mechanical ambushes) around their perimeter. MAs were claymore mines attached to trip wires. The devices provided extra security by blasting the enemy if the VC tried to sneak into the defensive perimeter. Division policy required infantry units to emplace the claymores nightly.

The previous night, the platoon, on orders from battalion, occupied positions inside the vee formed where two streams joined. During the night the floodwaters surged, and by the time the acting platoon leader realized the danger, the claymores, which were submerged and impossible to find in the blackness, driving rain, and swift current, posed a deadly threat. Afraid of triggering the unseen MAs, no one dared to move.

The flood swept nearly all of the soldiers downstream, many clinging to air mattresses. Non-swimmers attempted to climb trees, and most succeeded. The platoon lost many of its weapons, including machine guns, claymores, grenades, and grenade launchers. The radios, too, disappeared, along with several of the soldiers' packs. When morning arrived, the sergeant and one of his men hiked about three kilometers to reach LZ Stinson.

After hearing their story, I climbed aboard a chopper and began searching for the missing platoon, referring to a map that bore little resemblance to the lake-like scene below. Eventually, the pilot spotted a floating body—one of the missing soldiers. I reached out the door as we hovered, hauled the body on board, and continued the search. Three more bodies floated in the flood, nearly a mile downstream from the NDP.

As we progressed downstream, survivors perching in trees waved frantically when we passed over them. Stranded in hostile territory without weapons or food, the soldiers desperately needed help. The VC missed an opportunity to inflict terrible losses, but the flood restricted their movements too. We hauled the bodies back to the firebase and returned to rescue the treed soldiers.

With the rescue complete, I had time to think about the events that led to the disaster. The former company commander had been wounded and evacuated a week earlier. The executive officer, acting as company commander, operated with a different platoon and couldn't reach the missing platoon because of the flood. The battalion commander or his operations officer had ordered the platoon to its unsafe position, although I never figured out why.

The brigade commander relieved the battalion commander of command for ordering the platoon to occupy the ground near the river junction, and for failing to act when informed of the missing platoon. He also relieved the battalion operations officer of his duties. I have always wondered what action the battalion commander could have taken. Sending a recon patrol into the flood would have risked drowning more troops. The platoon had already lost its equipment and four men, although the commander didn't know that when I first arrived on LZ Stinson and reported to him.

The disorganized platoon remained on LZ Stinson. I joined another platoon and began rebuilding an effective fighting force from the shambles of my company as the wind blew away the remnants of the storm.

Years later, while reading an article by Al Hemingway in the November, 1995, issue of VFW Magazine, I discovered that perhaps our attempt to flood enemy territory up north had enhanced the storm. During a top-secret weather modification experiment named Operation Popeye, U.S. aircraft dropped "cloud seeding paraphernalia." The operation resulted in an exceptionally long and wet monsoon season, which forced the enemy to evacuate seventy American prisoners of war (POWs) from North Vietnam's Son Tay POW camp, twenty-three miles west of Hanoi. The POWs left the compound roughly two months before the unsuccessful American raid that attempted to rescue them. The one hundred U.S. Army Special Forces raiders didn't learn that the POWs had been moved until the raiding force landed at Son Tay in helicopters on November 21, 1970

Six weeks earlier, in South Vietnam near LZ Stinson, four drowned soldiers provided mute evidence of our success in reinforcing nature.

LZ Stinson as seen from Hill 85.
December 1970

Chapter 4

Sapper under the Hooch

Three days before the deadly storm hit Chu Lai, we new arrivals attended a class about sappers (suicidal enemy soldiers who toted satchel charges, wormed through perimeter defenses, and blew things up).

We were strangers, brought together for training at the Americal Division's Combat Center on the beach at Chu Lai, and the odds of us meeting again were slim. A few of us were launching our second tours in Vietnam, but most were newbies. All of us—combat arms officers, aviators, and members of support branches—were there to learn the common skills needed for survival during our tour of duty. After completing the day's training, we returned to the officers' barracks, swallowed a couple of beers, and swapped a few yarns before turning in.

The buildings, with wooden floors, sheet metal roofs, and screened sides, wouldn't stop a pellet from an air rifle, much less a bullet from an AK-47. Double bunks, arrayed along each wall and down the center, occupied most of the floor space. I chose a top bunk in the center row and went to sleep.

A commotion woke me around 0200. "There's a sapper under the hooch!" someone shouted.

Startled from a deep sleep, I looked, listened.

"I see him, too," someone else said. "He's carrying something!"

We had no weapons. Those would be issued when we arrived at our units.

Some officers swarmed in circles, like ants hurrying to protect an anthill. Others awoke and stumbled toward the doors. One idiot turned on the lights.

"Where is he?"

"I don't know."

"I don't know either. Who saw him?"

I decided, to hell with it. If a sapper had crawled through the wire and walked two miles or so across the base, bypassing helicopters and ammo dumps to single out our barracks on the beach, I figure he lacked the intelligence to light a fuse. Besides, I occupied the top bunk and had one warm body, two mattresses, and a floor between me and any explosion from under the hooch. I lay there half asleep.

In the midst of much scurrying around, one of the calmer officers looked under the building, which stood on piers above the sand dunes. When he reported seeing nothing, attention turned to finding whoever had seen the sapper in the first place. When the man who slept in the adjacent bunk pinpointed him—a sheepish-looking helicopter pilot—he admitted he had been dreaming, and that he often talked in his sleep. The other guy who had claimed he also saw the sapper decided that he probably had seen a shadow. Everyone went back to bed except me. I hadn't left my bed in the first place.

Time passed, and I went on to command Charlie Company. After a firefight that wounded two men, I requested a chopper so I could leave the field and visit them in the hospital. I remained in Chu Lai overnight to catch up on some administrative details. The next morning, I couldn't commandeer a chopper for the return trip to the field.

Charlie Company Sign in Chu Lai.

I called a friend, another captain, who worked at the Division Logistical Operations Center.

"Pete, I need a chopper ride to LZ Stinson to rejoin my company. Can you help me out?"

He could. Within an hour I was airborne en route to my battalion's firebase, with Pete along as a sightseer.

When the pilot turned his head to talk to his copilot, Pete punched me on the shoulder. "It's him!"

"It's who?"

"It's him, the sapper-under-the-hooch guy."

Pete, who had trained with me at the Combat Center at Chu Lai, had been particularly amused by the sapper incident.

I looked at the pilot, who turned to look at us, and sure enough, he was the officer who had caused all the commotion.

"You're right, Pete. That's the guy. What do you think we ought to do with him?"

The pilot attempted to shrink in his seat, wishing he were somewhere else. Then he had to explain the incident to his copilot, who couldn't conceal his eagerness to get back and tell the other pilots. Our pilot was not happy.

The chopper suddenly dropped, leaving our stomachs somewhere above. We shot across rice paddies, popped over trees at the last possible second, banked sharply around hills, skimmed the tops of rice-straw huts, and in general had the hell scared out of us.

When we arrived at LZ Stinson, I thanked the pilot for the ride, told him to look out for sappers, climbed out on shaky legs, and wished Pete luck on the ride back.

He told me later that the return trip scared him beyond belief. For the rest of his tour, he carefully identified each pilot before he boarded a chopper. He said he didn't have enough clean pairs of undershorts to last him through another ride with "Sapper Joe."

Chapter 5

Ya Gotta Speak the Lingo

There it is." I turned quickly, expecting to see something of real importance. Seeing nothing unusual, I turned back to the NCO I was interviewing. Getting to know my men on my first day as commander of Charlie Company, I had made a statement to this sergeant who, agreeing with me, said, "There it is." Only a few days "in country" on this tour, I had to master new jargon.

Each war in our history developed its own slang, and the Vietnam War was no exception. Slang from the streets attached itself to the duffel bags of the draftees and spread throughout the army, but other slang originated "in country," the term for being in Vietnam.

Slang from other wars flavored the speech of Vietnam-era soldiers too. "Bought the farm," a holdover from World War I, was a slang expression meaning someone had been killed. That term originated when the mortgage insurance paid upon the death of the mortgagee enabled the beneficiary to claim ownership of the property. Therefore, the soldier's death literally bought the farm for the beneficiary.

Terms used when referring to the enemy included "gooks," a holdover from the Korean War. A more common term for the enemy, at least where I served in Vietnam, was "dinks." I didn't know the origin of that term, but I suspected it might have had its roots in the Vietnamese language. The Vietnamese words for crazy are *dien cai dau*. Of course GIs couldn't be bothered with pronouncing each word correctly, so crazy became "dinky dow." Dinky, shortened to dink, referred to the enemy, and sometimes to the Viets in general. Another possibility was that the term derived from dinky, the English word that means "of small size." Because the Vietnamese were small in stature, dinky could be applied to them.

An "FNG," for f—ing new guy, was any man who had recently arrived in country. Seasoned troops also called the new soldiers "cherries." Experienced infantrymen avoided FNGs as much as possible because the new troops, unaccustomed to watching for booby traps, could stumble into tripwires and cause those around them to suffer from the explosions.

"Old Asia hands" were soldiers who'd already served a tour there.

Infantrymen referred to anyone who was not in the field with them as a "REMF"—rear echelon mother f—er. A relative term, it was used at each echelon to denigrate troops who were more remote from combat than the men using the derogatory label.

Slang or other terms varied somewhat depending on the unit or the geographical location in which the unit operated. Infantry slang differed from that of aviation units, and the slang of "Saigon warriors," those support troops who lived and worked in South Vietnam's capital, differed from that of troops who served "up country."

When infantry soldiers heaved their heavy combat packs onto their backs, they usually grunted from the effort. Consequently, they called themselves "grunts." They took a perverse pride in that name, for soldiers in no other branch of the army could be called grunts, although that term also described marine infantrymen.

Lieutenants, whom the troops called LTs (pronounced "Elltees"), led platoons.

Because I was the commanding officer, the initials of which are CO (pronounced "CeeOh"), that's how I was called, as in, "Hey, CO, there's Ho Chi Minh tracks over here." Enemy soldiers made rough footgear from old truck tires, and the tread made distinctive prints on the muddy jungle trails. That footwear became "Ho Chi Minh sandals," named after North Vietnam's leader.

When a soldier said something was "number ten," he meant it was pretty bad, as in "CO, these C ration ham and lima beans are number ten." Few things were worse than number ten, although some troops used the term "number ten thousand," often shortened to "number ten thou'."

"Bodacious" indicated something really impressive, as in, "LT, I just found a bodacious weapons cache." Soldiers from southern states used the word more often than northerners did.

Because we frequently talked over radios, many of the terms used in radio communications crept into our routine language. We said, "Roger that," to indicate agreement with the person who was speaking. The term came from the approved radio term "Roger," meaning, "I understand."

When an ambush patrol wanted to communicate silently with platoon headquarters, the radiotelephone operator (RTO) "broke squelch" at predetermined intervals by merely pressing the transmit key twice on the radio. The platoon leader would hear a brief rushing noise from his radio, twice, and know the patrol was awake and OK.

In an attempt to confuse any listening enemy, RTOs and leaders often used jargon while transmitting. Maps were "funny papers," streams became "blue lines," roads were "red balls," and we referred to friendly Vietnamese as "little people." Jet fighters were "fast movers," and the LOH-6, one of the helicopters that made up a helicopter gun team, was "the little bird." The AH-1G Cobra gunships that accompanied the little bird were "snakes."

When my troops sighted an enemy soldier and requested permission to open fire, the answer was often "Blouse him" or "Waste him," meaning, "Kill him."

When plans went awry, it was a "SNAFU," for situation normal, all f—ed up.

If things got really screwed up, apparently out of control, the troops said the situation was "FUBAR," meaning f—ed up beyond all recognition. Perhaps not unique to this war, it certainly was applicable in many instances.

A selector lever on the M-16 rifle allowed a soldier to select either semi-automatic or full-automatic fire. Instead of saying "automatic," the troops coined the phrase "auto-get-'em." When they switched their weapons to auto-get-'em, firepower increased dramatically. "Rock-and-roll" was another term we applied to weapons fired in the automatic mode.

Infantrymen didn't carry packs; they "humped rucks." A line of troops weaving through the jungle, humping rucks, followed their "point" and "slack." The first man in line, the point man, looked for trip wires and booby traps, and searched for a possible trail.

The second man, the slack man, looked farther ahead, searching for enemy bunkers or snipers in trees. Slack provided backup for the point if they came under fire.

If the troops received fire, and someone was killed in action, or KIA, he was "wasted." Of all the terms the troops originated, perhaps this one described best how they felt about the war and the men who died fighting in it.

Soldiers used another term that expressed their feelings about the senseless deaths of young men in their prime: "It don't mean nothin'." That expression helped them mask their feelings and move forward into the next battle.

Many of the enemy's hand grenades were made in China, so those grenades were "Chicoms," derived from Chinese communist. Those grenades weren't quite as lethal as our grenades, primarily because they didn't have as much metal in them. Nevertheless, the concussion from exploding Chicoms killed many of our soldiers.

American hand grenades became "hand frags," a shortening of the proper term "hand fragmentation grenade." That term avoided confusion with grenades fired from an M-79 grenade launcher by a "thump gunner." The noise the launcher made when the grenadier pulled the trigger gave birth to that descriptive term.

Shrapnel—steel fragments released when a grenade, mortar, or artillery round exploded— became "shrap metal."

Infrequently, disillusioned soldiers killed or attempted to kill their leaders. The method of choice was to toss a hand frag next to a sleeping officer or NCO. The soldiers called those murders or murder attempts "fraggings."

When a soldier was wounded I called for a "dust-off," or medical evacuation helicopter (medevac). The blinding, choking dust raised by the whirling blades of the UH-1 Iroquois chopper (Huey) spawned the dust-off moniker. A soldier medically evacuated by helicopter was "dusted off," although that term eventually referred to anyone who had been wounded, regardless of the means of his transportation to the hospital.

Dust-off helicopters were "slicks," they weren't gunships. Hueys that carried troops on Combat Air Assaults (CAs) were also called slicks, although they did carry two M-60 machine guns that door gunners fired from the open doors on either side.

To assist in navigation through unfamiliar terrain, especially in the jungle, I called the firebase and requested a "nav round." In response, the artillerymen fired 105 mm white phosphorous artillery rounds, or "Willie Pete," which burst in the air and gave me a target on which to sight my compass. From that known point I could determine my location. Often the "arty party" (artillery party) requested the navigation rounds for me. The arty party consisted of the artillery forward observer (FO), his NCO, and an RTO. The arty party traveled with my command group most of the time, responding to and relaying my requests for artillery fire.

Artillery Supported Charlie Company from LZ Stinson.
December 1970

After an infantry unit transmitted the required information when requesting artillery fire, the firebase let the calling unit know the request was being processed by saying, "Wait. Out." That term entered everyday lingo and meant that a request was being acted upon, or that someone was busy but would get to the request after a brief delay.

Once the firebase artillery officer had processed the request for fire and was ready to shoot, he transmitted, "Shot. Over." That meant that the infantry would see the rounds explode on the target shortly. Often the FO would turn to the infantry commander and say, "On the way. Wait."

Troops received their reassignment orders approximately one month before they were due to go home. When their orders arrived the soldiers said, "On the way. Wait," meaning they would return home soon.

Losses resulting from the war created an acute demand for leaders. The army initiated a short, intensive leadership course for NCOs, and unit commanders rapidly promoted graduates of the course to staff sergeant. Troops called these young leaders "Shake 'n Bakes," after a popular ready-mixed fried chicken seasoning that shortened meal preparation time. Soldiers also called them "instant NCOs." One of my finest NCOs was a Shake 'n Bake, which validated the program's effectiveness, at least in his case.

Like soldiers in previous wars, we ate combat rations, or C rations, or "Cs," but we also ate "lurrps." Long range reconnaissance patrols—LRRPs—had to be self-sufficient for long periods. C rations were heavy, so to reduce weight the army adopted the new, at the time, freeze-dried rations, issuing those meals to the LRRP teams. The rations became known as lurrps.

The men heated water over heat tablets, or "heat tabs," a candy-bar-sized, blue/white compressed substance that burned with a hot, blue flame. They mixed hot water with the lurrps and let the mixture soak for about twenty minutes. The soldiers heated cans of Cs over heat tabs too. The smell of hot instant coffee cheered us during the wet of the monsoons, but the burning heat tabs smelled like plastic and chlorine.

Approximately once every two or three months, we went into a three-day "stand-down" back in Chu Lai, the American Division's combat base. Stand-down offered a chance to relax, watch a Filipino floor show or two, eat steak, drink beer, swim in the South China Sea, or maybe call home via the Military Affiliate Radio System (MARS). During stand-down, the soldiers didn't "even" have to stand guard. The use of even, always emphasized, pervaded every conversation, as in, "CO, that dink fired a burst at me and didn't even hit me."

With his tour nearly completed, a soldier became a "short-timer," or "short." That term meant that he had little time remaining in country. Throughout his tour each soldier could tell his buddies exactly how many months he had left in "the Nam," and as he got short he began to count the number of days left to serve. When his remaining days dropped from one hundred to ninety-nine, he became a "double-digit midget." Finally he began to count the hours, saying, "I'm too short to smoke a long cigarette," or "I'm too short to start a long conversation." The ultimate in being a short-timer was when he could say, "I'm not short, I'm next," meaning he would be the next soldier in his unit to depart for home.

Finally, a Vietnam veteran "DEROSed." Date expected to return from overseas was the magic date. If a soldier hasn't been dusted off or wasted, on his DEROS he boarded the "Freedom Bird" and "crossed the pond" to the "world" or the "Land of the Big PX."

Chapter 6

The Villes

We called them villes, short for villages. The number of hooches, or dwellings, in a village didn't matter—they were all villes. If the tiny villages appeared on a map, we frequently referred to them by their Vietnamese names, altered to match the soldiers' ability to pronounce them.

On the coastal plain that stretched from the South China Sea to the Annamite Mountains, the soldiers of Charlie Company named the scattered villes in terms that recalled ville-connected events, or described the huts and their inhabitants. One of the most hostile villes was Tra Binh Dong, which we called Dodge City.

Charlie Company rode into Dodge City, not on cow ponies but in helicopters. Consisting of a series of separate clusters of two or three hooches located among rice paddies and bamboo thickets east of LZ Stinson, Dodge City erupted in a shoot-out each time the Americans rode into town. We didn't stride down Main Street while challenging the bad guys to come out and fight fair. No, we dived from our choppers and took cover behind the nearest paddy dike, knowing the showdown would occur at a time and place chosen by the outlaws. The VC shot from ambush, often disappearing without a trace before we could unholster our massive firepower. We saw lots of gun smoke, but we never did find Matt, Kitty, or Doc.

Peasant woman making rice flour in "Dodge City."
January 1971

The term dink often referred to friendly Vietnamese as well as to the enemy. We applied that name to one village. We first swept into that collection of five hooches at daybreak, after a sleepless night in which we moved twice to avoid enemy mortar fire. A short time after we had moved from our night defensive positions, mortar rounds crashed onto the former locations, events that quieted the complaints of the tired soldiers.

Passing the first hooch, the point man surprised two black-pajama-clad VC, a man and a woman, walking across a rice paddy. He yelled, "*Lai day* (Come here)."

The VC spun around, racing for the bamboo-and-grass shacks located across the paddy. We opened up, killing the man, but the woman escaped, disappearing into the cluster of hooches. We searched diligently, but we never found her. Instead, an old woman staggered screaming from one of the huts, blood washing down her back from the glancing impact of a stray M-16 bullet. I called for a medevac chopper.

Shortly thereafter, a middle-aged, one-legged man herded a water buffalo into the paddy, bracing himself on a crude, hand-hewn crutch. Clad in black pajamas identical to those of the dead VC lying a short distance away, he commenced plowing.

That ville became the One-Legged-Dink Ville, a site we returned to several times. On each occasion, the one-legged Vietnamese farmer ignored us after his initial restrained greeting. His ability to traverse the rice paddies, following the water buffalo while gripping the plow with one hand and the crutch with the other, amazed me. Equally proficient in planting and harvesting the rice, he stood on one leg, working with one hand while he grasped his crutch with the other. He devoured American C rations with similar alacrity.

Basket Ville consisted of two hooches and a large earthen bunker, surrounded by spiky bamboo. The friendly family that lived there spent their days weaving split bamboo into baskets, which they sold or bartered. For some reason we never drew fire from that ville. Perhaps the VC didn't want to endanger a source of tax revenue.

Nhan Hoa, a large ville of more than two dozen hooches, squatted at the foot of a mountain crowned by OP George, an observation post. We spent Thanksgiving Day in that ville, delighting in the waterfall that tumbled from the heights above. It provided our first shower in a long time. Hot food, flown to us in insulated containers aboard a helicopter, offered a wonderful change from C rations.

Some villes consisted of several widely separated clusters of straw shacks. Cartographers assigned numbers to the individual clusters, but one name sufficed for the entire ville. An Diem 2, for example, was the ville along the Tra Bong road where we once ran into an ambush. An Diem 3 was away from the road, and other villes followed the same numbering pattern. We referred to those villes collectively as the An Diems, the Thach An Nois, and the Vinh Locs.

Booby Trap Alley stretched between the Thach An Nois and One-Legged-Dink Ville. More nightmare than ville, it consisted of a series of hooches and trails scattered among trees and hedgerows that concealed the VC. The enemy fired from ambush, then disappeared. If we pursued, we hit mines and booby traps. I eventually avoided Booby Trap Alley entirely. The few kills we made there weren't worth the casualties we suffered. I'm sure a labyrinth of tunnels ran underneath us while we patrolled above, but we seldom found them.

The Thach An Nois and Vinh Locs, collections of hooches scattered along rice paddies interrupted by tree-covered knolls, savaged us. Thick vegetation concealed booby traps and snipers, a combination that took a terrible toll of Charlie Company's troops. Prohibited by unreasonable rules of engagement from calling indirect fire into those villes, we fought, cursed, suffered, and died.

Among those who survived, the memory of the men maimed or killed near those rude collections of grass-and-bamboo huts remains. The names of the villes don't matter anymore.

Charlie Company headquarters in patrol base in Booby Trap Alley. December 1970

Searching huts in Ngoc Tri. December 1970

Chapter 7

A Night Combat Air Assault

Fierce enemy fire pinned down one of my platoons in Dodge City, and I was too far away to give urgently needed help. Thick vegetation that surrounded me muffled the rattle of automatic weapons and small arms fire, but grenade bursts told me that the platoon was in close contact with the enemy.

My company headquarters occupied an NDP in a densely wooded area in what we called the High Ground north of LZ Stinson, two kilometers from the erupting battle. Because the company operated as widely separated platoons, the platoon I accompanied couldn't reach the engaged platoon and add its firepower to the battle.

The platoon leader radioed, requesting a medevac helicopter. Although still under heavy fire, he had to evacuate his wounded. I called the battalion Tactical Operations Center (TOC) and requested a dust-off chopper.

The battalion commander, with me in the field for a night—for the only time during my months as a company commander—stood nearby, listening. I planned to conduct a forced march in the darkness to reach the beleaguered platoon. Instead, the battalion commander called the 198th Infantry Brigade and requested helicopters for a night combat assault, a rarity in the Americal Division in 1970–71. With the request approved, we prepared a one-ship PZ (pickup zone). I activated my strobe light as the first chopper approached. Feeling vulnerable to snipers, I held the blinking light in the middle of the clearing that was surrounded by dense, black forest. The pilot, guided by the light, inched his chopper down between the trees. I handed my strobe light to the platoon leader, and my headquarters group scrambled aboard, leaving heavy packs and a small security force behind. Our lift bird rose into the dark sky as the next ship approached the PZ.

Circling overhead while waiting for the remainder of the choppers to pick up the rest of my troops, I talked over the radio with the harassed platoon leader, who described a two-ship LZ located between the platoon and the enemy.

When we arrived, the LZ blazed with streams of tracers crisscrossing the treeless paddy. This would be a hot one. Ready for the assault, as my lead chopper flared into the LZ prior to landing, I cautioned the pilot to instruct his door gunners to fire only from the left door. Gunships rocketed the hedgerows and bamboo thickets just ahead of us, throwing dirt and splinters of bamboo high into the air amid the orange-red flashes of the exploding munitions.

As the helicopters touched down, we dived out the left door and provided suppressive fire for the departing and approaching choppers, raking the hedgerows with grazing fire, forcing the enemy to take cover. The noise, a melding of whirling chopper blades, rattling machine-gun fire, exploding grenades, rifle fire, and the blasts of rockets and 40 mm rounds from the gunships, threatened to burst our eardrums. A circling C-130 flareship (Moonbeam) illuminated the area, and behind us a hay fire in a barn-like structure glowed red and angry. The odors of burning hay, gunpowder, and smoke from smoldering bamboo raked our nostrils and stung our eyes. Thousands of tracers arced through the night and ricocheted from the ground, trees, and paddy dikes. The glowing bullet paths resembled red whips lashing repeatedly to punish the recalcitrant darkness. I found the stressed platoon leader, located his platoon's positions, and withdrew the newly arrived platoon toward the barn and huts. Slammed by the overwhelming firepower of two platoons and the gunships, the VC called it a night. The fight ended.

An injured cow, silhouetted against the glow of the smoldering hay, moaned her agony into the night. Shrapnel had sliced into her back and blood oozed from a dozen wounds. She shuffled her feet but remained standing.

The battalion commander stayed with us until daybreak, and then called for a chopper to transport him to LZ Stinson. The rest of us began another day of seeking the enemy, starting with a search for bodies. Blood trails indicated enemy casualties, and we estimated six VC killed or severely wounded.

Because no choppers were available, the soldiers I had left behind on the PZ the night before struggled with our rucks and theirs, weaving through trees and thick underbrush in the furnace-like heat. They descended from the High Ground and onto the open coastal plain, arriving in mid-afternoon, joining us as we engaged in another firefight in a different cluster of huts.

Because we were low on ammunition and because I needed an aerial view of the situation, I requested a chopper, and to my surprise I got one immediately. The battalion commander was sleeping, and the operations officer sent me the commander's bird.

The chopper landed while under fire, picked me up and flew me to Stinson, where I loaded rifle and machine-gun ammo aboard. Upon returning, I could see the platoon below heavily engaged with the enemy. After we circled so I could assess the situation, the brave pilot landed in the middle of the firefight without hesitation, and we delivered the ammo. I remained on the ground, ducking bullets and trying to determine the enemy's exact location.

The platoon leader informed me that he urgently needed a dust-off. His platoon sergeant, peering around the side of a hooch, had attracted the attention of an unseen sniper. The VC shot the soldier twice in the head. I requested a medevac chopper, doubtful that the wounded man would survive. He died in the hospital two days later.

The fight ended soon after we evacuated the wounded NCO. It had been a long day, starting at daybreak thirty-six hours previously. We needed sleep, and apparently the enemy did, too. No one fired a shot that night in Dodge City.

Chapter 8

The Man in White

Deep wrinkles furrowed his brow and cheeks. He shuffled, cumbered by his years. Ivory thatch and goatee complemented his white shirt and trousers, contrasting with green bamboo hedge and brown paddy. He was barefoot. Puttering near a hedgerow, he waved and watched as we—alert and cautious—traversed a fallow field.

Charlie Company had conducted a helicopter combat assault into a nearby rice paddy two nights before, where we reinforced a platoon fighting off a fierce attack near some grass shacks in Dodge City.

After that battle, and after the firefights that followed, we swept the neighboring fields and hedges under a sweltering sun, searching for the Viet Cong who usually triggered a gunfight in and around Dodge. The VC honeycombed the ville with spider holes and tunnels; finding them all proved impossible. We destroyed those we found, but on each ramble through Dodge we encountered new burrows and fresh enemy soldiers.

Enemy automatic weapons fire crackled, digging up the ground around us, driving us to cover behind the nearest paddy dike. The firefight intensified as we fought back with rifles, machine guns, and grenade launchers. I forgot about the man in white, concentrating instead on staying alive and defeating the enemy. The brief fight ended, inconclusive, with no friendly losses. We would search the distant tree line for evidence of enemy casualties.

Advancing toward the enemy-occupied hedgerow, I flinched as heart-wrenching wailing wavered across the paddy. Turning toward the sound, I glimpsed a bent old woman hobbling toward the trees to my left, arms stretched in front of her as if pulled by an invisible cord. She threw herself onto the ground, disappearing behind the trees and shrubs.

I remembered the man in white standing near those trees, and with ugly suspicion tormenting me I changed direction, striding to the tree line.

Beyond the trees, arms wrapped around her dead husband, the widow vented her anger, her grief, her despair. She screamed, she bawled, she sobbed, and finally she whimpered, sinking into the emptiness of a future without her mate. Her tears diluted a red splotch that merged with others as his blood seeped from multiple bullet holes in his shirt, transforming his white clothing to crimson.

Our eyes met. I shuddered at the anguish and intense hatred surging across the abyss that separated us. Her feelings needed no common language to bridge the distance from her soul to mine. Unable to withstand such intensity, I shifted my gaze to the dead farmer. As if he had known the end was near, and had welcomed it, his wrinkled face was serene. Choked with emotion, I whispered, "I'm sorry," and turned away.

The hapless man's strange reaction, standing upright in full view and waving when caught in the middle of a firefight, mystified me. Whether he attempted to draw our attention away from the VC's position I can't say. Perhaps he tried to warn us. The poor peasant died as he had lived, with dignity and calm acceptance of his fate.

The man in white became just another number in a war where inflated statistics enhanced or destroyed careers. Uncertain as to which side caused his death, I reported him as a VC killed in action. He probably was a VC, at least when the Viet Cong controlled his village. When we won the shoot-outs, he became a friendly Vietnamese farmer. Without the means to change his circumstances, he changed his loyalty. I couldn't blame him for that.

I turned for a final look at that huddled heap of human misery and then walked away, toward the next hedgerow and the next firefight.

Chapter 9

Saved by an Air Mattress

Charlie Company's command group and the first platoon plodded upward as dusk began to displace the day's heat. A gentle breeze masked the soft rustle as jungle-fatigue-clad legs nudged aside weeds and small bushes while the soldiers leaned into the hill against the pull of their heavy packs.

Near the top I stopped, switched my M-16 rifle to my other hand, and gazed back down the hill and into the shadows that nearly obscured the rice paddies we had just waded across. I saw nothing unusual and turned to scan the hilltop. The soldiers' heavy breathing interrupted the silence, and someone coughed. The troops eased sore muscles under the pack straps that cut into their shoulders through sweat-stained fatigue shirts, and some soldiers turned their eyes toward me.

"Check out the other side of the hill and establish security," I ordered in a low voice. The nearby acting platoon leader, a sergeant, responded, and the company began to move into a night defensive position. To keep any enemy observers off balance, the company often set up an NDP, and then moved after dark to an alternate location. By moving into NDPs late in the evening, I occasionally allowed the company to stay in one position all night. Tonight I planned to stay put, and whispered my plan to my RTO.

The RTO grunted with relief as he removed his rucksack and radio, loosened the straps that secured his air mattress to his pack, and, with cheeks bulging, blew up the mattress. I was tired, hungry, and looking forward to a little sleep, and I moved to a position five yards from the RTO's location, where I shrugged my shoulders from beneath my combat pack straps. A low sound behind me disturbed the quiet evening.

Pop. Hiss.

"Aw, shit."

The RTO whispered mild curses as air escaped through a puncture in the tough rubber air mattress. The resupply chopper had delivered a new air mattress to him yesterday. Tonight he'd again sleep on the sun-baked ground. I chuckled and stepped closer to the RTO.

"What did you lay it on, a bamboo thorn?"

"I don't know, CO. I was just about to take a look."

The RTO lifted the limp air mattress from the ground, peered through the semi-darkness, and froze. Three stiff wires protruded from the sandy soil a few inches from his left boot. I squinted in the dusk, spotted the telltale sign of a bouncing betty anti-personnel mine, and shuddered. No longer could I whisper; Charlie Company headquarters occupied a mined hilltop.

"Nobody move," I ordered. "Do not move from the exact location you now occupy. We're in a mine field."

Bouncing betty mines had a small charge that, when the trip wires were disturbed, shot the mine about three feet into the air. At that height the main charge exploded, sending shrapnel into the torsos of anyone within the bursting radius of the device. The Viet

Cong buried the deadly mines along trails, in hedgerow openings, and on observation points such as hilltops.

If the unit attempted to move from the hill in the dark, the chances were high that someone would step on a mine. In the rapidly fading light, picking out the tiny wires that betray the mines' locations would have been impossible. And perhaps there were other types of mines. Decision time.

It was a gamble, but remaining in place until daylight seemed to be the best course of action. I informed the other platoons of the situation, told the men around me to get as comfortable as possible while remaining in place, and settled in for another long night. Dawn was light years away.

At daybreak, the soldiers picked their way down the far side of the hill, each stepping carefully in the footprints of the man in front of him. When the last man reached the relative safety of the field below, grenadiers fired grenades from the their M-79 grenade launchers, targeting the hilltop. Two secondary explosions resulted, underscoring the unit's incredible luck. A punctured air mattress saved the platoon and company command group from disaster.

The RTO added an air mattress to the company resupply list. I added a special, "Thank You," to my nightly prayer.

Chapter 10

On the March

The point man, first in the long line, moved cautiously. Point men tied their jungle-fatigue trousers tightly to their legs to prevent the swish of loose cloth against leafy vegetation. Some claimed they'd be able to feel an unseen tripwire against their legs if their pants clung to their skin. Alert, silent, moving into the unknown, they earned their comrades' admiration and gratitude.

Mid-column, my company command group advertised its location with radio antennas swaying above the RTOs. The end of the column looked to the rear, guarding against an attack from that direction. Healthy men assisted straggling soldiers who, weakened by malaria or recovering from minor wounds, couldn't keep up with the main body. Accordion-like, the column expanded and contracted, undulating toward the next firefight. We approached a river that intersected our route across the coastal plain.

River crossings were dangerous operations that required planning and caution. Guards spread out to protect the vulnerable river crossers against enemy snipers. A sergeant stripped to his shorts, swam across the river, and strung a rope from bank to bank, creating a lifeline against the strong current. With their arms and hands encumbered with the tools of an infantryman, and with their heavy packs pulling them off balance, the soldiers struggled to stay on their feet in the brown, swirling water. All troops crossed safely, and the enemy, if he was hiding in holes along the banks, remained unseen and unwilling to fight.

Crossing a river near Tra Binh.
November 1970

I could smell dinks on occasion, which aided in avoiding an ambush or leading us to a recently abandoned enemy position. The odor, a mix of sour rice and old fish, was quite easy for me to detect, although few of my troops were able to identify it. I sniffed about like a bloodhound near the riverbank, but all I smelled was the faintly musty, pungent odor of my canvas pack.

We moved quietly through the trees, heading away from the river. The squish, squish of soggy boots following one another down the trail created an aqueous rhythm, a liquid accompaniment to the ragged beat of marching feet. We approached an open area where we would receive a resupply helicopter. The pace quickened.

"Pop smoke!"

The pilot of the in-bound Huey had radioed and asked me to mark the LZ with colored smoke. My RTO pulled the pin on a smoke grenade and tossed it into the center of the clearing.

"Smoke's out," I told the chopper pilot.

"Roger, I got your goofy grape," he replied.

"Affirmative on the goofy grape," I said.

Because the VC knew about our habit of marking a landing site with smoke, enemy soldiers sometimes tossed smoke to lure pilots into an ambush away from the real LZ. We had learned not to identify the color of the smoke we would use until after the pilot saw and named the color.

The chopper landed and off-loaded mail, rations, and other supplies, and then lifted off in a cloud of dust and disappeared into the afternoon sun.

Sitting on steel helmets turned upside down to accommodate their buttocks, soldiers read letters from home. Barefoot, hatless, drying their soreness in the sun, they escaped their miseries for a short time while words of loved ones spoke softly from scented pages of letters always too brief. Eyes glistened unnaturally in the sun's glare and focused on photographs of wives and sweethearts, children, and parents. Other soldiers, those whom the mail chopper disappointed, stood guard, cleaned their weapons, brewed coffee, or pretended to doze while concealing their dejection. They wondered when the next mail bird would arrive, and if they would be one of the lucky ones. Meanwhile, they dreamed of a land that grew more perfect as the days went by, a land so far away that the only measurement of distance was time. How many days left in this land of booby-trap-dragons and mine-monsters, its air frequently filled with steel and lead? They wondered how they could spot the dragons, avoid the monsters, dodge the metal.

The sweet, home-cooked smell of chocolate chip cookies yanked at my heartstrings when I opened a care package from home. I opened an envelope of lemon-scented instant tea, dumped it into my canteen cup, and added water from my canteen. Tea and cookies. Life was good. I saved the raspberry Kool-Aid for the next day.

The leaders distributed C rations, the troops tucked their precious letters away in watertight plastic bags that once protected new PRC-25 radio batteries, and the medics examined and treated sore feet. Grunting and groaning under packs now full of heavy cans of rations, extra ammunition, hand grenades, claymore mines, and flares, the infantrymen of Charlie Company continued their day's work, marching toward the jungle-covered mountains and the next engagement with the enemy. The sun sucked sweat from every pore, but at least the mosquitoes took a break. The biting swarms would return in force when night fell.

Night smothered the jungle with a suddenness that was astounding as the sun plunged into the mountains. Mosquitoes swarmed, injecting the darkness with an incessant hum that maddened us. Head nets protected heads and necks from the tiny attackers, and mosquito dope smeared on hands and around boot tops kept the critters hovering just inches away from sweaty bodies, at least temporarily. Even with the best protection available, some mosquitoes penetrated our defenses and stabbed our skin.

Malaria was a constant threat, and we swallowed one small white pill daily and a large orange pill weekly as a precaution against two types of malarial fever carried by the buzzing mosquitoes. Even so, some soldiers caught the disease because they failed to swallow the pills or forgot to smear themselves with insect repellent. And some deliberately tried to catch malaria as a way to leave the field and avoid any more combat.

Jungle nights suffocated our senses. Peering into the surrounding vegetation was like closing my eyes inside a dark closet while trying to inventory its contents. False images soon appeared, drifting across my mind, causing fear and excitement. Was that really something moving out there, or was it my imagination? Was that object there a few seconds ago? What was that noise? Should I order my troops to throw grenades? Pop flares?

Nights in the jungle were endless, a suspension of time and space, filled with crawling, biting insects, snakes, blood-sucking leeches, and fear and decay and threat of death.

Demands of command interrupted the long nights. Because my RTOs, working in shifts, repeatedly awakened me so I could clear artillery fire into my area of operations, sufficient sleep eluded me. Harassment and interdictory fire (H&I) denied the enemy unchallenged use of suspected rest areas and supply routes along remote trails. Artillerymen on LZ Stinson targeted trail junctions and clearings, but first I had to verify the grid coordinates and confirm that no friendly troops patrolled near the impact areas. Night after night I granted permission to fire, then lay awake while bursting shells shattered the stillness.

On other nights, I accompanied a platoon that I had ordered to raid a village that intelligence reports claimed harbored VC, or I coordinated fire support for a separate platoon engaged in battle. When the enemy attacked our positions, usually at night, no one thought of sleep. Therefore, I slept when I could, taking brief naps, day or night. After nights of heavy combat action, I declared a day of rest—that is, provided the enemy also took the day off, or I didn't receive orders to move to some distant location in reaction to a nebulous intelligence report.

My men slept no more than I. They had to perform perimeter guard duty, lie alert in ambush sites, or conduct night raids on suspected VC villages. Sleep became a precious interlude, and I fantasized about an uninterrupted night of it, in a bed, safe from ground attack and the savage bursts of enemy mortar fire that ripped the night apart.

Gradually, then with increasing swiftness, daylight flooded our positions, expanded the known, and pushed back the unknown and the imagined. Night fears surrendered to the day, replaced by a heavy pack and the furnace-like heat of the merciless sun.

A faint clink sounded, announcing the locking of a canteen cup handle. A soldier prepared to heat water for a cup of instant coffee on a stove handmade from an empty C ration can. He rummaged through his pack for a can of C ration ham and eggs, chopped, while he waited for the water in his cup to boil. The rustle of his searching reminded other troops that they had survived one more night in the Nam.

Chapter 11

Keep Your Head Down

G radually, one bullet at a time, the bond developed. Forged in the crucible of combat, tempered by raw courage and tested by shared fear, it strengthened with each firefight. Infantry combat could be a lonely, personal ordeal for an FNG. A soldier new to his unit, new to combat, experienced loneliness and fear that could paralyze. Good leadership and peer support overcame his desire to dig a hole and hunker down, praying the bullets would miss and the mortar rounds wouldn't explode.

His leaders guided him, but the green soldier turned to peers to help him over rough spots. A hand reached out and offered a cigarette or a cookie sent from home. Grateful, the new man accepted. The lives of seasoned veteran and scared replacement would soon depend on each other. Country bumpkin or streetwise hood, college grad or high school dropout, they faced death or disfigurement side by side. Education and social status were meaningless when the air snarled with whizzing shrapnel.

"I'm Tom. Sarge send you over?" The veteran had just started to dig a foxhole.

"Yeah." The cherry, in clean, dark combat fatigues that contrasted with Tom's faded, filthy uniform, removed his pack and unsheathed that miserable little shovel the army called an entrenching tool. Its paint was unblemished.

One stood guard while the other labored. They spelled each other, the digger trusting the guard to remain alert.

"Looks deep enough. Whaddaya think?" Dirt smeared the scarred blade of the FNG's new infantry shovel.

"Yeah, that's OK. You dig a grenade sump?"

"Yep."

"OK," the old hand said. "Now let's put out our firing sector stakes. Sarge'll be by shortly."

They settled into the foxhole. The veteran sat, opened a C ration can of hard crackers. The replacement constantly wiped his hands on his pants, checked his ammo pouches, tapped his fingers on his M-16 resting on the loose dirt that formed a frontal parapet. The veteran's teeth crunched the crackers. The sun plowed into the trees. Mosquitoes hummed and stung. The new guy cursed softly. "Damn bugs. Got any bug dope?"

"Here. Keep it. I got two."

"Thanks." He smeared the greasy liquid on his neck, face, and arms. He looked at the small plastic bottle stuffed under the camouflage band on the vet's helmet, then slid his bottle beneath his own camo band. He peered through the dusk, relying on his ears when his eyes failed him. He shivered, even as sweat moistened his hands and oozed from beneath the sweatband on his helmet liner.

Mortar rounds slammed into the trees fifty yards away, shredding the silence. A small fire flickered where the rounds impacted, casting a faint glow. The old hand reached up, grabbed the newbie's jungle-fatigue shirt. "Get down, you damned fool!" He hauled his new foxhole buddy down beside him.

"They're attacking!"

"Not till the mortars quit. Keep your head down."

The men listened to the distant thump of enemy mortar rounds leaving the tube, then cringed as the blast of the impacting shells roared past, rippling earth and air.

A pause followed the thunder. "OK, get ready."

Together they rose, thrust their rifles over the parapet, and squinted through the darkness.

"Remember your aiming stakes. And squeeze 'em off."

"You scared?"

"Damn right. Don't mean nothin'. You want to live, you fight." The combat vet eased the safety off. "Now shut up."

AK-47 fire ripped past, high. The wavering line of steel sounded like corn popping. Somewhere to their right a friendly opened up, hosing the shrubbery with an M-16 on full automatic. "Damned fool ain't seen nothin' yet. Don't you pull that shit."

The new man strained to sort out shadows from enemy. "There. Left of that big tree. He's crawling this way."

"Yeah, I got him. Good eyes, fella. Shoot."

The newbie's finger squeezed the trigger.

"I got him! Did you see him drop?" His first kill.

"No. Look right of that same tree. Let's waste 'em."

The battle intensified. Calls for a medic, shouts of anger and fear, the roar of exploding claymore mines, and the pop and sudden white light of flares combined to numb and confuse. The infantrymen's tracers zipped open the darkness, pouring steel into the crawling enemy. And the veteran steadied the newbie, kept him alive and effective. The rattle of rifle fire diminished, died away.

"See any more? I think they quit." The replacement's voice was high, shaky.

"Don't count on it. You OK?"

"Yeah. What time is it?"

"Don't matter. You got a year to do, so what difference does it make? You ain't goin' nowhere."

Dawn slithered through the trees, encroaching on the darkness.

Helmeted heads peered over the parapets. A medic scurried along the defensive perimeter, checking the wounded. An infantry-man groaned in the next hole. Bandages swathed his head; only his nose protruded from the gauze turban.

"Tom?" The newbie called the veteran by name for the first time.

"Yeah?"

"Reckon they'll be back?"

"Naw, not in daylight. Smoke?"

"Thanks. Can I make coffee now?"

"Go ahead. Heat enough water for me, too."

Expended brass clinked underfoot. Cigarette smoke and the ac-rid odor of the heat tab burning in a homemade C ration-can stove rose above the foxhole. Water boiled in the canteen cup. The newbie poured half into Tom's cup and dumped in a packet of instant coffee.

"Here."

"Thanks. Got any sugar?"

"Yeah, here." He handed Tom an individual packet.

"You done good last night. Figured you'd waste a whole lot of ammo, but you didn't. Must've had a good sergeant during your ad-vanced infantry training."

"Meanest bastard I ever met. Can I ask a question?"

"Go ahead." Tom flicked his cigarette butt out in front of the foxhole. It landed among a cluster of empty brass casings. A thin line of smoke rose from the butt, hanging in the still dawn air. A dead enemy soldier, mouth open in a silent scream, lay twisted and broken just beyond the glittering brass. "What's your question?"

"How come you ain't got a foxhole buddy?"

"He got dusted off day before you got here."

"Bad?"

"Bad."

"Damn. Sorry 'bout that."

The silent veteran gazed at the dead Viet Cong. The new man stared into his canteen cup.

"Tom? We going to be foxhole buddies?"

"Don't see why not. I can't sleep and stand guard at the same time."

"Tom?"

"What, for chrissakes?"

"My name is Dan."

"OK, Dan. Keep your head down."

Chapter 12

Flu, Mines, Rats, and Snipers

Towering cumulus clouds ambushed the sun. The wind increased, rattled the bamboo, rippled the rice paddies in its rush across the plain. Fifty-caliber-bullet-sized raindrops rat-tat-tat-ed against my helmet, soaking me in seconds. The monsoon season arrived, and at first I welcomed the coolness. However, within a day or two I was cold except when on the move. Damp, penetrating chill soaked into my core. Who said it's always hot in Vietnam? Did the enemy suffer from the weather as much as I? I hoped so.

My head ached, my bones ached, I had an unquenchable craving for water. I knew the signs; flu germs had launched an all-out attack. I asked my company medic for medicine to relieve the misery that grew stronger, diluted my strength.

As dusk approached, we halted. I struggled from my pack, grateful that my weakness hadn't overcome me while on the march.

I bent over to open my pack just as shrapnel whizzed past, inches from my head. I heard the bang and the scream at the same time, and I rose from where I sprawled to see a soldier writhing in pain near a bamboo clump. On his back, he flailed the surrounding grass with his arms, seeking relief from terrible agony. An enemy bouncing betty mine, buried near the base of the bamboo, amputated his leg just above his boot. The blast shredded his other leg, his arms oozed blood from dozens of shrapnel punctures, and his face was a bloody mess.

I called for a dust-off chopper, we loaded him aboard, and then I prepared for another night in the cold, cold rain. His buddy buried the wounded soldier's boot with the foot still in it. I ached from fever, but the pain paled compared to the ache in my heart for the wounded soldier. I doubted that he would survive.

The endless rains lashed, chilled, immobilized us. The rivers rose, making crossing them impossible. We hunkered down, content to remain in one location, knowing that the weather restricted the enemy too. The constant wet wrinkled our skin, and infection from an unknown source caused one of my big toes to swell. When we eventually moved again, the infection spread, enlarging the toe to the size and color of a plum; when I walked, it throbbed with pain. My medic recommended that I go to the firebase so the battalion surgeon could examine the toe.

A chopper transported me to LZ Stinson, where the surgeon lanced the toe, draining the pus and relieving the pressure. He told me to remain on the base for two days to let the healing begin before I again slogged through stinking rice paddies fertilized with water buffalo dung and human feces.

While I healed in a bunker on the firebase, the surgeon and the battalion chaplain constructed a blowgun from a length of half-inch steel pipe, using hypodermic needles as darts. We declared war on the extensive rat population, and vented our frustrations by blowing darts at the foraging rodents. They reminded us of the elusive Viet Cong, difficult to see and hard to corner. Occasionally we hit one, and added a tick mark to our rat-body-count scoreboard. Most rats were, of course, identified as VC rats—that is, except the huge ones. Those monsters were labeled North Vietnamese Army (NVA) rats, and we entered their deaths in the NVA column.

Just before I boarded a chopper to return to the field, a runner called me to the battalion TOC. I hobbled to the bunker, where a duty officer informed me that one of my platoon leaders had been wounded, and a dust-off chopper was transporting him to a field hospital. As the lieutenant had been guiding his men into an NDP, an enemy sniper had shot him in the knee. I directed my chopper to take me to the evacuation hospital, which was merely a series of Quonset huts clustered near the Chu Lai airfield.

I stood next to his bed, watching the lieutenant struggle awake against the anesthesia. Still groggy, he attempted a grin. He looked around, remembered. The grin faded, and he asked if his knee would be all right. I reassured him, although I doubted he'd regain his former skill as a basketball player. A bloody tube extended from thick bandages that wrapped his knee, which appeared to be the size of a basketball. The tube drained into a large stainless steel receptacle that was half filled with bloody fluid.

I squeezed his hand, wished him luck, and said goodbye, turning quickly away so he couldn't see my tears. I stumbled into a nurse, who asked if I was OK. I nodded and limped to the door, unable to speak.

Why had I lost so many platoon leaders and soldiers, yet remained unscathed myself? Survivor's guilt depressed me. I fought it, telling myself that my time could come at any moment. I boarded the chopper and returned to the field where I belonged, once again leading my soldiers.

The rains stopped.

Chapter 13

The High Ground

It rose abruptly from the coastal plain, a menacing, jungle-covered island amid a profusion of rice paddies and hedgerows. I called it the High Ground, with capitals, because I came to know it well as commander of Charlie Company.

Reacting to an intelligence report, we waded through the hush of a waist-deep swamp en route to the High Ground. Supposedly, elements of the 48th Viet Cong Battalion occupied positions beyond the swamp, in a secluded ravine. The swamp offered a concealed, muted approach to our objective, away from the watchful eyes of villagers to our left and the noisy route through scrub and jungle on our right.

Suddenly the artillery forward observer's sergeant started bitching. "This is stupid. Ain't no enemy in a goddamned swamp. Why in hell are we wading through this shit when we could walk around it on dry ground?"

A weak NCO, he complained frequently and in large doses.

I sloshed toward the rear of the column, rippling the leek-green surface scum into small, angry waves. His lieutenant attempted to silence the man, with no results.

"Sergeant," I said as I reached him, "shut up."

"There's probably snakes in this water. Why in hell are you making us walk through this swamp?" he said.

I grabbed a fistful of his jungle-fatigue shirt as I stood nose-to-nose with him. I hissed, "Sergeant, if you open your mouth one more time and endanger the lives of the men in this unit, I'll have you court-martialed for disobeying a direct order. You'll finish your tour in LBJ—as a private," I said, referring to the stockade near Saigon that we called Long Binh Jail. He quit talking. I slogged back to the front of the column, furious that an NCO would display such behavior.

I motioned for the leader of the platoon that I accompanied to join me, and he, his platoon sergeant, and I had a brief chat. I wanted to be certain of our location before leaving the swamp.

"Lieutenant," I said as we studied my map, "I think the objective is just over that low ridge," pointing to a tree-choked ridge at the end of the swamp. Dense stands of vine-entangled trees smothered the surrounding terrain, making precise navigation difficult.

"I agree, Sir," he said. "And thanks for shutting that man up."

The platoon sergeant concurred with our estimate of our location, and we trudged out of the swamp, where we again halted. Then the lieutenant, the platoon sergeant, my company RTO, and I crept forward to reconnoiter the objective. The sound of voices and the strange discord of Vietnamese music rose from the ravine below. A series of immense boulders leaned against each other, forming grottoes and sheltering the small stream that trickled through them. Somewhere in that confusion of moss-covered rocks and crannies, enemy soldiers felt secure enough to play a radio.

Hoping to avoid hand-to-hand combat in the confines of the boulders, I withdrew beyond the ridge and radioed for helicopter gunship support.

"Lieutenant, spread half your platoon along this ridge," I told the platoon leader, "then deploy some men across the stream down there as a blocking force." I pointed to an opening perhaps seventy-five meters downstream from the last of the rocks. "We'll see what happens when the gunships arrive."

I took care to keep the artillery sergeant behind the ridge, out of hearing range of the enemy. Now that we faced combat, his attitude had changed noticeably. His eyes widened, he kept checking his weapon, and he seemed ready to flee at the first shot. "Lieutenant, keep an eye on this man. And keep him quiet," I told the FO.

When the gunships arrived, I threw a yellow smoke grenade in front of the boulders, marking the target. "Firebird Zero Four, this is Ramrod Tasker Six," I called to the lead gunship pilot. "Friendlies are downstream fifty meters from the smoke and also on the ridge to the south. Target is unknown number of Victor Charlies in rocks about twenty-five meters upstream from the smoke. Make your gun runs upstream only. Identify smoke. Over."

"Tasker Six, I've got yellow smoke. Over."

"Affirmative on yellow smoke. You are cleared in hot. Clearance initials Lima Bravo," I told him, giving him my initials, LB, as required before gunships could fire close to friendly troops. Clearing him in hot meant that I had authorized him to fire his rockets and grenades as he made his approach to the target.

The rockets exploded into the boulders, sending shrapnel in all directions, but I doubted if the fire was having the desired effect. Ordering the gunships to cease fire and orbit while we assaulted, I gave the order to attack, and the platoon leader and several of his men charged into the stacked boulders. My radio operator and I went with them.

Automatic weapons fire burst from the rocks, and a Chicom grenade landed in front of us. The platoon sergeant picked it up and threw it back into the boulders, where it exploded. He and the platoon leader rushed forward, throwing grenades and firing their M-16 rifles. The enemy fire slackened, but bullets still whiffed past us, ricocheting from rocks and trees.

The gunship lead pilot called me. "Tasker Six, this is Firebird Zero Four. You've got bad guys running up the ravine away from you. Looks like six of them, maybe more. Over."

"This is Tasker Six. Blow 'em away. Clearance initials Lima Bravo. Out." The gunships passed low over us as they made their gun run, then blasted the ravine with rockets and 40 mm grenades.

"Tasker Six, this is Firebird Zero Four. Looks like one body in the stream, maybe another one in some brush. Rest of them scattered into the trees to the northwest. Over."

I acknowledged, telling Firebird to orbit while we charged into the boulders again. This assault was uneventful.

To prevent more of the enemy from escaping into the woods across the ravine, we fired M-79 grenades into the trees, denying them that escape route. I instructed the gunships to place suppressive fire into the ravine upstream from the boulders. The chatter of small arms and the thumps of the outgoing M-79 grenades made a ragged rhythm, while the crack and boom of rockets and 40 mm grenades, compressed between the walls of the ravine, added emphasis to the interrupted cadence. The enemy quit shooting. Our fire dwindled, then stopped. Water from low, dark clouds replaced the rain of bullets. The gunships returned to their Chu Lai base.

With darkness only an hour away, I ordered my unit to withdraw to a night defensive position on the hill above the boulders.

I sent a small force back into the ravine to search among the boulders in the dying light. They reported finding a large weapons cache, indicating we had located the enemy battalion's weapons company, the one that frequently mortared LZ Stinson. Mortars, rocket-propelled grenade launchers, AK-47 and SKS rifles, and ammunition for the weapons lay in crevices and niches throughout the boulders.

I ordered M-79 grenades to be fired into the ravine at odd intervals throughout the night to prevent the enemy survivors from returning and retrieving their weapons. The exploding grenades and soaking rain made the night seem endless. No one slept.

At daybreak I sent a larger force into the boulder complex, and we spent the entire day hauling captured weapons to the ridge, where we cleared a landing zone, then loaded the enemy weapons onto choppers for transport to LZ Stinson. A few enemy bodies lay strewn along the ravine, including the Viet Cong RTO and his radio, but the driving rain had obliterated any blood trails.

The boulder complex offered a convenient sanctuary for the enemy, and I had no doubt the VC would use the grottoes after we left. I didn't want to have to dig the enemy out of the boulders again, so I asked the battalion operations officer to send out some powdered tear gas. The resupply chopper brought a 40-gallon barrel of CS, a persistent chemical agent that would remain for weeks. Several soldiers carried the heavy container down into the ravine and into the boulders, and one of my sergeants wrapped detonating cord around the barrel and lit a long fuse. The explosion shot powdered tear gas throughout the complex, and I was satisfied that we had denied the enemy one hiding place for a long time to come.

We heaved our packs onto our backs and began the long trek through the High Ground along a trail that led to Dodge City.

The High Ground viewed from Dodge City.
December 1970

Americal Division commanding general awards Captain Lee Basnar a
Bronze Star for valor for action in the High Ground. A platoon leader and
platoon sergeant received Silver Stars in the same battle.
October 1970

Chapter 14

Monkey and Twoey Louie

Kids, lots of kids. Barefoot, dressed in shorts and black shirts, kids seemed to be everywhere. We encountered them in the villages, in the paddies, and in the hills. GIs couldn't resist befriending kids. We fed them, treated their sores and bruises, and played games with them during breaks. They toted sodas and beer in packs on their backs, or they balanced a case of Coke on a bicycle seat and wheeled the bike for miles until they found us. Kids sold the warm refreshments for a dollar a can. The price was a bargain to a thirsty GI. We were tired of drinking contaminated water that tasted like iodine from the purification tablets we had to drop into our canteens or risk hepatitis or dysentery or some other disease.

When the kids disappeared we braced ourselves, knowing that the enemy was close and combat would soon erupt. Seldom did we encounter kids older than twelve. At that age they either fought against us as Viet Cong or plowed the fields and paddies, replacing the man of the house who had left his family to go to war, just as I had left mine.

Twoey Louie joined us near Dodge City on South Vietnam's coastal plain in late 1970. While we conducted a sweep, looking for the elusive Viet Cong, the kid appeared on a trail, smiling and asking for "chop chop" (food). Subsequently, irrepressible Louie appeared whenever we swept through his hamlet. He spoke no English, yet he communicated well with the soldiers of Charlie Company.

The lad, eight or nine years old, unconsciously rubbed a narrow 2-inch-long scar on his right cheek. The ring finger and little finger on his left hand, welded permanently together, told of previous contact with what was possibly white phosphorous or napalm. The rest of his fingers on that hand were missing. We called him Twoey Louie because of his maimed hand and remaining two fingers. The top part of his right ear was gone, probably the result of the same mishap that scarred his hand and face.

Monkey (left) and Twoey Louie heat water for
LRRP rations near Dodge City,
February 1971

Louie had an older friend whom I dubbed Monkey. The boy's long arms and simian facial features suggested that moniker. Monkey, ten or eleven years old, didn't always appear with Twoey Louie, which made me wonder if the older lad was busy setting booby traps for us to trip over.

The two boys had no schedule. They spent the days and nights with us, moving with the troops until we reached the lads' self-imposed boundary. Then they waved good-bye, watching us through the wavering heat until we disappeared.

Despite suspicion that they passed information about us to the VC, we couldn't resist feeding them C rations and playing with them during breaks. They enjoyed the jokes the troops played on them, and they devised mischief of their own. If a soldier napped during a break, the two young Vietnamese loved to tie the laces of the unsuspecting infantryman's right and left boot together.

"Monkey," a Vietnamese boy, one of Charlie Company's two mascots.
February 1971

Both boys were knowledgeable about our weapons, and a few soldiers allowed the lads to clean their M-16 rifles for a pittance, usually paying them with C rations or a dollar's worth of military payment certificates (MPCs). Each man checked his weapon thoroughly after the boys finished their job. The industrious little guys also blew up our air mattresses in return for food. We began to view Twoey Louie and Monkey as our company mascots.

Monkey wandered off one day, stumbling along in an old pair of GI combat boots that were several sizes too large for him. I never saw him again. Louie remained with us, choosing to bed down near me in my company headquarters group.

We stopped near a two-hooch ville, a couple of bamboo-and-straw shacks hugging the edge of a field that stretched to the low, brush-covered hill 300 yards from us. An old couple lived in one of the shacks and used the other to store their meager tool supply. Perhaps the former occupants of the tool shack had been killed, inducted into the South Vietnamese Army, or were members of the local 48th VC Battalion.

I chose the tool hooch for my command post. Our radio antennas outside pinpointed my location to any enemy scouts, although my RTO usually attempted to conceal the antennas in overhanging tree branches, if there were any trees available.

Seated beside me outside the hooch in late evening, my RTO transmitted our night locations to battalion while Twoey Louie, squatting next to me, heated C ration beans and franks over a heat tablet. The tomato-and-bean aroma of the Cs curled past my nose while I composed a letter to my family. My thoughts turned to my daughter, about Louie's age, safe at home in the States. They were two kids, born on opposite sides of the world, their childhoods as different as the political views of North and South Vietnam. Given the chance, I bet Lorraine and Twoey Louie would have become friends.

A burst of AK-47 fire splattered the ground around the three of us as we sat exposed beside the straw hut. Twoey Louie scrambled into my lap, interfering with my dive for the hooch and its meager cover. "*Toi so qua, Dai Uy!* (I'm terribly afraid, Captain!)," he shouted. I untangled myself from Louie and both of us dived behind the hooch while bullets smacked into the bamboo poles and hissed through the straw over our heads. The hut wasn't good protection, but it offered concealment.

My RTO landed beside us, leaving the radio exposed. I retrieved it, then told my forward observer to call for a fire mission. Within five minutes artillery rounds slammed into the hillside across the open field, and the bullets stopped cracking and snapping around us.

Twoey Louie's eyes were as big as the bottom of a C ration can as he trembled and clutched my leg in the dusk; a little boy surrounded by foreigners, being shot at by his own countrymen. Like the war itself, it didn't make sense.

Chapter 15

A Noisy Country

The noises of Vietnam assaulted my ears the moment I arrived in-country. At the busy Bien Hoa Air Base, I watched and listened to a big C-130, which carried a full load of ammunition and other supplies to be delivered to Qui Nhon. The high-pitched whine of the airplane engines stabbed my eardrums as the C-130 taxied to the end of the Bien Hoa Air Base runway, twelve miles north of Saigon. The whine changed to a roar as the Hercules lurched forward, gathering momentum, struggling to lift its heavy load in the tropical heat.

Chu Lai, the huge American Division combat base hard against the South China Sea, rattled with the beat of medevac choppers hauling their loads of broken, shattered soldiers to the surgical and evacuation hospitals. The clatter of helicopter gunships, lifting from Chu Lai airfield to carry their deadly loads into battle in the paddies, jungles, and mountains to the west, resounded across the base from the rhythmic slap, slap, slap, of the whirling blades.

Aircraft noise from both planes and helicopters was only a part of the racket that assailed my ears during my tours in Vietnam. Away from Chu Lai, out where the infantryman earned his meager pay, the noise became more intense, louder, more personal.

Twenty-five kilometers southwest of Chu Lai, LZ Stinson, fire support base for the 1st Battalion, 52d Infantry, pumped artillery and mortar rounds into the surrounding hills and fields. The boom of the outgoing harassment and interdictory (H&I) fire was a loud, comforting sound, soon followed by the crrrrump of the rounds impacting distant, usually unseen, targets.

Three-quarter-ton trucks growled their way from the LZ Stinson chopper resupply pad to the mess tent near the top of the hill, hauling foodstuffs for the cooks to turn into a meal for support personnel as well as the infantrymen who guarded the base.

Generators underscored the cacophony with their steady hummm, providing the electricity to power lights, radios, and other equipment.

Helicopters landed and departed from the helipad on Stinson, with the huge CH-47s (Chinooks) transporting the supplies and munitions required to support an infantry battalion in combat. Their slapping blades caused hurricane-like winds, filling the air with dust and the whistle of the turbines.

After a brief stay on LZ Stinson to refit and take our turn guarding the firebase, we usually went back to the field aboard UH-1 Iroquois helicopters. These ubiquitous Hueys lifted the fighting troops from Stinson to our objectives, usually a rice paddy, a small field next to a cluster of grass shacks, or a jungle clearing. The line of Hueys radiated their blades' whop, whop, whop throughout the valleys, causing the humid air to reverberate with the telltale sound of impending assault.

As we made our final approach to a landing zone, the booms of the impacting artillery rounds rolled away from us as the artillery shifted fire, making way for either Cobras or C-Model Huey gunships to roll in hot, blasting the LZ with rockets and 40 mm rounds. The sharp crack of rockets launching from gunships slapped against unprotected eardrums, causing unprepared soldiers to wince from sudden pain. The impacting rockets spoke with a deeper, authoritative bang, punctuated by the pop, pop, pop of exploding 40 mm grenades.

The M-60 machine guns on the troop-carrying Hueys commenced firing, their rattle replacing the diminishing slap, slap, slap of the now-orbiting gunships. The Huey blades, their pitch shifting to a sharper whap, whap, whap, sliced the air, dispersing the drifting smoke that partially obscured the LZ.

Sometimes the LZs were cold and we landed without taking fire. But sometimes the whip-crack of enemy AK-47 bullets ripped the air as we dived from the hovering choppers and sought cover behind rice paddy dikes or clumps of bamboo. The sharp crack, crack of the M-16 rifles returning the enemy's fire became the chorus, soon joined by our machine guns tapping out the refrain. The thump, thump of the outgoing M-79 grenades added an unsteady, hesitant beat to the combat concerto.

Occasionally cries for a medic grated on nerves already stretched and raw. Radios crackled, sergeants shouted, and high overhead, heard only during brief lulls in the awful noise, a command-and-control helicopter maintained a faint, steady beat with its whirring blades.

If the battle increased in intensity, U.S. Air Force jets screamed overhead, circling while their forward air controller dived toward the target, the engine hum of his OV-10 Bronco interrupted by the thud of the white phosphorous rockets striking the target.

The jets screamed down, one following the other, dropped their bombs, then roared skyward as their afterburners powered them away from the green tracers that stabbed the sky around them.

The unbelievably loud booms of the detonating bombs rolled across the battlefield in huge shock waves, drowning the whip-crack of enemy AK-47s.

Sometimes a C-47 (Spooky; or Puff, the Magic Dragon)—an air force twin-engine transport modified to carry guns and flares—circled the action, its rapid-fire cannons ripping down upon the enemy in a loud, long buuuuurrrp. Tracers formed narrow streams of red, liquid fire, hosing the enemy positions with thousands of rounds of ammunition.

Shrapnel from grenades and mortars snarled, whizzed, and zipped past, decreasing as the grunts' firepower poured into the enemy positions. If a dust-off chopper approached, the ground fire built to an insane crescendo, with infantrymen launching withering small-arms and automatic-weapons fire, forcing the Viet Cong to take full cover and cease firing while the chopper recovered wounded soldiers.

The rapidly beating blades of the medevac Huey resembled the sound of a subdued machine gun amid the shouts of soldiers. When the medevac had successfully lifted off, the firing often dwindled, creating a lull until the enemy again picked up the pace. The battle noise would continue, rising and falling, abusing the air, slamming against our ears, until the enemy broke contact and retreated to lick his wounds. A loud silence followed. After such a battle, my ears rang like a roomful of unanswered telephones.

The orbiting helicopter would depart to refuel. Not a bird chirped; no one spoke. Then the static of a radio breaking squelch would bring me back to the job at hand, and the faint rattle of equipment as soldiers moved to better positions would remind me of consolidation, resupply, and other chores that demanded my attention in the strange quiet that descended on Charlie Company.

Chapter 16

Not Every Cobra Was a Gunship

The point man crept along the jungle trail, alert for snipers and trip wires. Dense foliage restricted his view to a few feet.

Thump! A huge snake dropped from a tree, landing just in front of the startled soldier. As the snake slithered toward him, he identified it as a cobra, as deadly as the Viet Cong who occupied the jungle stronghold.

He jerked the trigger of his M-16 rifle and blasted a hole in the cobra near its tail. Now the snake raised its hooded head higher, writhing, lashing, propelling itself toward the retreating infantryman. He fired another burst into the snake, and the reptile coiled around itself in its death convulsions, no longer a threat.

I heard the shots up ahead and called for a situation report, expecting that my soldiers had killed a sniper. Instead, the patrol reported one VC cobra KIA.

The heavy, seven-foot long snake, perforated by bullet holes, would have meant agonizing death for anyone whom the snake might have struck. We didn't know why the cobra was so aggressive, but its actions symbolized that entire mission—nature's unusual response to our invasion of the jungle.

The company, transported by helicopters, had landed just short of the jungle's edge. During the ensuing two weeks we found few VC, but the jungle inhabitants made up for a lack of enemy soldiers.

We waded upstream in a jungle river until it narrowed, spilling between walls of a steep ravine. Jungle menaced on both sides, blotting out the sunlight. Mountains loomed beyond the stream, soaring to several thousand feet. The terrain guarded its secrets closely, daring us to continue. An ambush here would be disastrous; perhaps there was another way.

Sloshing downstream, the point man found a narrow ravine leading to higher ground. After I struggled up the steep riverbank I paused, catching my breath while I leaned against a vine-wrapped tree. One of the vines moved, inches from my hand.

A three-foot-long, light-green bamboo viper, sometimes referred to as the Cambodian Two-Step, slithered slowly along the branches over my head. Staggering backward, off balance under the weight of my combat pack, I pointed out the deadly viper to the next man in line. He drew his machete from its scabbard and hacked the snake's head from its body. We probed deeper into the jungle.

When the sun set, we halted in the suffocating heat and prepared defensive positions amid the rotting vegetation, which released a fetid, ancient odor, suggesting danger and disease and death. While I prepared my sleeping position, I saw a nearby soldier jerk backward. I hurried to him, thinking that a snake had bitten him. I was wrong. While the private unpacked his combat pack next to a dense clump of bamboo, a krait crawled from the roots, poised to strike. This small viper, two feet long, gray, with darker diagonal bands, is as deadly as a cobra. The soldier severed the snake's body with his machete as the light faded from the humid jungle.

Before going to sleep, I removed my boots in an attempt to dry my feet, which were a mass of sores from constant immersion in rivers, rice paddies, and monsoon rains.

I awoke at dawn, felt something sticky on the bottom of my right foot, and looked down to see two leeches dangling from it. Engorged with blood, the bloated leeches resembled fat, black cigars. I held the flame of a cigarette lighter near them and they dropped, squirming in the damp jungle soil.

Leeches are not poisonous, but the wound they create is easily infected. When a leech bites, it injects an anticoagulant to prevent clotting while it sucks its victim's blood. The substance keeps the wound open, oozing constantly. My foot leaked blood for three days.

I saw two more leeches undulating across the ground, their heads erect and swiveling, reacting to my odor, which by now was pretty impressive. These hadn't fed, so they were only two inches long—skinny, dark, and slimy. I squashed them with my boot heel when they approached my sore feet.

Two mornings later, I turned my jungle boots upside down and shook them as part of my morning routine. A few ants fell to the ground. I slipped my left foot into the boot and immediately entertained the troops with a strange, one-footed, hopping dance. My foot felt as if it were being stabbed with a hundred needles. I snatched the boot off and discovered an ant colony that had taken up residence during the night. I hadn't shaken the boot vigorously enough. I did now, knocking the heel on a rock. Hundreds of ants spilled out, along with ant eggs and a jungle-debris nest.

More monsoon rains slammed into us that day, putting the finishing touches on a mission that was long on misery and short on results. Nature, like the enemy, attacked without warning.

We slogged out of the jungle under a lashing, driving rain. I conceded that round to nature, but I added three VC snakes and a half dozen enemy leeches to our body-count tally. I couldn't let nature declare a total victory.

Chapter 17

Rules of Engagement

Bullets smacked against the paddy dike, ricocheting past me, throwing clods of dirt into my face. I dived from the trail, hunkering behind the protective two-foot-high dike. My soldiers crouched in a similar posture on either side of me. My RTO's radio antennas attracted enemy fire like a latrine attracts flies.

I peeped over the dike to determine the source of the fire. More rounds zinged into the dirt in front of me, while others cracked and snapped overhead. I found the enemy's general location.

I directed my weapons platoon to put mortar fire into the tree-covered ridge across the dry rice paddy ahead of us. They responded well, placing accurate fire and silencing the enemy weapons. And I had just violated the rules of engagement.

We were prohibited from using indirect fire, such as mortar and artillery rounds, without getting clearance from our higher headquarters. We could shoot back with rifles and machine guns, which were direct fire weapons, and we did, but indirect fire proved more effective against an unseen enemy. At the headquarters, when staff officers received requests for indirect fire they scrutinized their maps; if the requested target area was colored red, no such fire could be approved. The "measle sheet" architects who colored certain areas red didn't consider the lives of my men. No, they worried about the lives of Vietnamese civilians and property damage.

Helicopter gunships were considered direct fire weapons, but the time it took to get approval to use them, and for them to arrive, often meant casualties. Once on station, the gunships wouldn't fire until I gave the pilot my initials, clearing him to blow away a hooch or other structure that was the source of the enemy fire.

If I called for gunships, I was prepared to authorize them to blow away any building that I suspected sheltered the enemy. With my soldiers' lives in the balance, I wasn't concerned about destroying a cluster of huts.

I respected the reasons for caution when returning fire, and I was reluctant to place fire into a village when we couldn't determine the exact location of the enemy. But lying in an open paddy, with bullets zinging overhead and hammering against a sheltering dike, gave one a different perspective from that of a policy maker sitting in an air conditioned office in Saigon.

On another occasion, we again came under fire while crossing an open field. The bullets seemed to come from an old wooden structure nestled in some trees. The building reminded me of a French villa, looking strangely out of place in the remote countryside. We returned fire, but were in a difficult position. We couldn't advance or withdraw without becoming excessively exposed. A second enemy automatic weapon joined the first, pinning us behind a paddy dike.

Denied artillery support, I called for gunships and gave my initials—Lima Bravo. The pilot double-checked to ensure that I had authorized him to blow away the villa. I confirmed, and the rockets blasted the old building and surrounding vegetation. The enemy fire ceased.

We advanced across the paddy and found an old man holding a dead chicken. Two wounded chickens lay bleeding at his feet. The exploding rockets had partly collapsed the porch roof, and a jagged hole gaped in one wall. Extremely upset, the owner still wouldn't reveal the enemy's location.

I felt sorry for him, but none of my men had been killed or wounded, and that was paramount in my mind. He had no choice but to shelter the VC. I had no choice but to protect my men. Such are the conditions of war.

The unreasonable rules for ground engagement that frustrated us matched the ridiculous rules for aerial target selection that frustrated the U.S. Air Force over North Vietnam. How I longed to get Defense Secretary Robert McNamara on the ground with me for twenty-four hours. Strange (which coincidentally was his middle name) how he completely changed his outlook twenty-five years later. He would have changed it a lot sooner had he joined the infantry under fire in a rice paddy.

Chapter 18

Convoy to Tra Bong

The village of Tra Bong huddled near the west end of a potholed dirt road that began at Highway 1. Jungle-choked mountains, scarred by bomb and artillery craters, rimmed the tiny valley, looming over the artillery firebase that occupied a small hill adjacent to the village.

The Americal Division sent convoys to Tra Bong once or twice a year to replace damaged artillery pieces and to demonstrate our ability to use the road. During the remainder of the year, the road's stewardship remained debatable.

The 198th Infantry Brigade commander selected me to command one of the convoys. Available assets included a combat engineer platoon, artillery and gunships on call, and an LOH-6 helicopter, referred to as a Loach, which I used for my command ship. A transportation corps lieutenant led the ground element, which consisted of twenty or so trucks, including one modified to mount .50 caliber machine guns on either side of its cargo compartment.

The engineers led the way, sweeping the road for mines. Light Vietnamese traffic, mostly bicycles and Lambrettas, suggested that mine risk was minimal, but the possibility of buried charges, command-detonated by hidden VC when a truck passed, concerned me. Tom, my pilot, and I scouted ahead of the convoy at low level, hovering at culverts and other likely mine locations, looking for wires, hidden VC soldiers, or any other signs of danger.

The trip to Tra Bong was uneventful. We exchanged artillery pieces, and the convoy started back. As we neared the village of An Diem 2, a helicopter gunship team, supporting an ARVN unit, engaged an enemy force just south of the road. The Loach that snooped at low level, locating targets for the gunships, received heavy fire and crashed, sending up a fireball that shattered any hope of survivors.

Meanwhile, I received a report that a South Vietnamese unit had sporadic enemy contact east of that location. Tom and I flew to investigate. En route, north of An Diem, I saw an NVA soldier talking with a woman in front of her hut, his tan pith helmet distinctive against the dark door opening of the straw shack. With enemy on both sides of the road, an ambush of our approaching convoy appeared certain.

As Tom flew me across the road at low level to check out the hedgerows and wooded area to the south, a B-40 rocket zoomed up at us, barely missing. Small arms fire, which we returned, came at us from various locations. Once we were back over the road, I radioed the lieutenant to halt the convoy in place and deploy security.

Higher headquarters denied my request for artillery support because we were in a red area on the measle sheets. The enemy could shoot at us with any weapon he chose, but in this inhabited area we could shoot back only with direct fire weapons. I requested and received helicopter gunships, but the team refused to fly close enough to the enemy positions to place accurate fire on them. The destroyed little bird, still smoking, had spooked the Cobra pilots; their fire was ineffective, which was unusual.

Daylight faded, and a night attack by at least one NVA company seemed certain. Each time Tom and I flew over the suspected ambush site, we drew fire. Artillery or a few low-level passes by the gunships would have neutralized that fire. Denied these options, the convoy would have to break through the likely ambush site on its own.

I attempted to tell the lieutenant to get rolling and discovered that his radio was inoperative. We landed. I briefed the lieutenant and told him that I would notify the rear of the convoy to follow him when he moved out.

We made a low, slow pass while, through the open chopper door, I gave arm signals to the drivers, motioning for them to begin moving. The lead vehicle made it through the heavy fire, but the gun truck took a direct hit from a rocket-propelled grenade, which severely wounded two engineers. The convoy halted, its route partially blocked by the damaged truck.

Tom again took us over the action at low level. Seeing room for the convoy to pass just north of the wreck, I motioned the drivers on. Tom landed the chopper in the darkness and intense fire, and we loaded the wounded men onto our Loach.

We lifted off amid incoming and outgoing tracers, flew the wounded to the hospital at the Chu Lai base, and returned to the convoy. The gunship support improved in the darkness, silencing the enemy fire with salvos of rockets. Above us, in layers, helicopters from brigade and division circled to watch.

After the final convoy vehicle had cleared the ambush site, I looked back to see artillery exploding near the enemy rocket launcher position. I welcomed the overdue support, but it came too late to help the two wounded engineers, one of whom died in the hospital.

Below us, under the light from artillery flares, dust raised by the convoy settled back onto the Tra Bong road, but the issue of who controlled the road still hung in the air.

Chapter 19

The Deer

The idling choppers, five in all, danced in the mirage created by the heat of tropical sun and helicopter exhaust. From a distance, my men appeared to sway in rhythm with the distorted, dancing choppers—a grotesque, olive drab reproduction of an image in a fun-house mirror. Only this wasn't fun.

Each soldier, nearly doubled over by his eighty-pound combat pack, needed a boost to board his assigned helicopter. The grunts, each a walking arsenal, were one-man killing machines. Weapons were their tools, and they knew how to use their tools effectively. When the last man had struggled aboard, the increasing speed of the blades as we departed Chu Lai airfield provided some relief from the fumes and oven-like heat, but not from the fear and tension that pervaded each lift ship.

In addition to the familiar quivering of excitement and fear deep within me, I felt the weight of command as the first bird—the one I rode in—lifted off and swung west, away from the coast and over even hotter terrain. Our objective lay on the coastal plain, a broad, flat area that stretched from the South China Sea to the forbidding mountains to the west.

Small clusters of mud-and-bamboo hooches speckled the plain, interconnected by bright green rice paddies and clumps of darker green, thorny bamboo. The flooded paddies mirrored the sun. Now disappearing into a bamboo thicket, now reappearing to reflect again from the surface of the rice-choked water, the sun kept pace with the choppers.

The dusty road leading from Highway 1 to the remote village of Tra Bong passed under us, its traffic clearly visible from our low altitude. A couple of three-wheeled Lambrettas weaved around the potholes and slowed as the thumping rattle of the passing helicopters reached the drivers' ears. Girls in their traditional *ao dais* pedaled their bicycles, their conical rice-straw hats protecting their faces from the sun, and from the eyes of the soldiers passing overhead. A small boy rode on the broad back of a large water buffalo, guiding the animal with a mere switch.

Beyond the road, the pattern of paddies, hooches, and bamboo continued. In the center of that primitive agricultural region, our objective, the High Ground, rose from the plain like an island, imposing, forbidding, dominating the region. I would lead Charlie Company into Landing Zone One—a small saddle between knolls—which I had selected from my knowledge of the area gained in a battle there a few months before. Choppers one, two, and three lined up for a landing in LZ One. Choppers four and five would land at LZ Two, another nearby clearing.

My feet dangled from the open chopper door as I sat on the floor and looked across the airspace to the helicopter flying slightly behind and to one side of my lead ship. I lifted my hand in a half-salute to one of my platoon leaders sitting in a similar posture. His chopper slowly rose and fell with the effect of the heat rising from the ground and from the turbulence created by my aircraft. I wondered if his stomach trembled as much as mine and wondered, too, if I transmitted my inner anxiety to my troops. I certainly hoped not. Leaders can't show fear.

The High Ground crept nearer, shimmering in the fierce heat, menacing, threatening. How many eyes were watching our approach, wondering where we would land, or if we would? My sweat-drenched, jungle-fatigue shirt smelled sour from heat and anxiety. Perspiration streaks, white with salt, ringed the armpits.

We would assault without a landing zone prep (a softening up of the LZs by artillery and helicopter gunships) because I wanted to take the enemy by surprise, or at least delay revealing our intentions until the last minute. The tactic was a gamble, but one I accepted. Gunships orbited overhead in the event the LZs proved hot (enemy-occupied). Artillery, aimed and ready to support us, offered additional firepower if needed.

The two LZs, now recognizable straight ahead, grew larger. About 500 yards apart, their distance allowed landing on one in case the Viet Cong occupied the other, yet the proximity permitted mutual support. To the north, the ground sloped from LZ One into a bowl filled with scattered trees and elephant grass. Beyond the bowl the terrain rose again prior to plunging toward the Tra Bong road. Near LZ One, a hill rose steeply for 700 feet, a jungle-covered, vine-matted threat. LZ Two—flatter ground farther from the hill—looked more inviting.

The chopper noise changed abruptly when the pilot slowed the chopper in preparation for landing on LZ One. "Here we go," I thought, "Let's get this thing on the ground fast." No infantryman likes that slow descent into an LZ. It is then that he is most vulnerable to enemy small-arms fire and rocket-propelled grenades.

The door gunner opened up with his M-60 machine gun, placing suppressive fire on the landing zone, just in case the enemy waited.

The machine gun's rattle added a staccato beat to the rhythmic slap, slap of the chopper blades. We continued the approach, unopposed.

I jumped from the chopper while still three feet from the ground, followed by my RTO and company medic. The weight of our packs drove all of us to our knees in the tall grass, and the RTO turned turtle from the extra weight of his radio. From his back, he stared up at me. Other members of my company headquarters group leaped from the opposite side of the lift ship, and we spread out as the slick gained altitude and departed.

I watched the second lift ship approach and shifted my attention to LZ Two. It too was cold (unoccupied), and I turned my internal anxiety down from extreme to cautious.

The consolidation went well, no enemy contact interfered, and we settled down prior to starting the patrols that would take part of the company up that steep hillside.

The patrols had a tough time slashing through the thick jungle on the hill, and nearly three hours passed before they broke out into an open area near the top. The soldiers found no signs of enemy activity, nor could they locate the underground hospital that intelligence officers had told us existed somewhere on the High Ground.

I remained in the saddle near the LZs where I could easily control the company, talking in hushed tones over the radio with my platoon leaders, plotting their progress on my map, sweating in the merciless sun, and looking frequently into the grassy bowl below me.

During the dry season my body, seldom dry, rebelled, stinking in the heat. A sour smell surrounded my neck, caused by the sweat that accumulated in the towel placed there to absorb it. My boonie hat smelled sour also, as did my jungle fatigues.

The chemical smell of burning heat tablets, mixed with the scent of instant coffee and C ration peaches, came from the vicinity of my RTO. I never did figure out how he could drink hot coffee in the smothering tropical heat.

Captain Lee Basnar sits in front of his poncho shelter in the High Ground.
February 1971

Several hours passed, boring, slow. Combat is like that—fear, intense action, relief, boredom—all mixed up in no particular order. Each day brought new fears, more boredom, and one less day to spend in that danger-infested country.

Smoke from a nearby rifleman's cigarette drifted my way. Moving to avoid it, I looked carefully for snakes in the tall grass. I came to a small mound that presented an excellent view of the bowl, and I sat, conscious of the damp odor of decaying vegetation and the hay-like scent of dry elephant grass. This was a country of contrasts and contradictions—beauty and ugliness, dryness and dampness, silence and ear-drum-rupturing noise.

Distant movement caught my peripheral vision. I swung the muzzle of my M-16 rifle in that direction and flipped the safety off, ready to kill what I thought was an enemy soldier.

Instead, a deer bounded erratically through the elephant grass, now in sight, now invisible. The waving grass telegraphed its progress, and I evaluated the possibility of venison steaks cooked over an open fire, replacing the tasteless C rations for at least one meal. Could I divide the deer into enough pieces to give every man a taste?

Closer and closer she came, swerving around obstacles not visible to me, but always closer. I sighted my rifle on a small opening in the brush and grass about sixty yards away. Perhaps the deer would come through that area and I could get a shot. My RTO stood nearby, eager for me to shoot.

The deer sprang into the clearing, took two smaller jumps, and stopped. She looked back over her right shoulder, presenting a clear target. I sighted on her neck, using the base of her left ear as my aiming point, and then slowly lowered my rifle. "Shoot, CO," my RTO whispered.

"No, something's wrong," I said. "Something spooked that deer. Let's wait and see what's behind her."

The deer leaped over a small bush, passed within thirty yards of me, and bounced out of sight. I stood up so I could see farther into the bowl.

Twenty minutes later the patrol on top of the hill called me. "Six, this is One. We have activity in the bowl to your north. Looks like one Victor Charlie with a weapon, moving southwest. Over."

"One, this is Six. Roger. Keep me advised. Out," I replied. I gave the handset to my RTO, only to hear the platoon leader calling again.

"Six, this is One. He's changed direction and is moving toward your location. Over."

"This is Six. I can't see him through the brush and trees. What's the range from your location? Over."

"This is One. About 900 meters. Over."

An M-60 machine gun had a maximum effective range of 1100 meters. "This is Six. Shoot him with your Mike-Six-Zero. Out."

A machine gun opened up, firing into the bowl from atop the jungle-covered hill. Tracers passed 150 meters in front of me, impacting into the elephant grass.

The enemy soldier burst into view barely 100 meters from me, running, dodging, desperate to reach the only real cover available to him: the mound I occupied.

The machine gunner, high on the hill to my left, had difficulty with the deflection caused by shooting downhill at a moving target, and the extreme range didn't help matters. The rounds impacted close to the enemy soldier, but failed to bring him down.

A commander seldom shoots. His job is to command, not fight as an individual rifleman. Usually when a commander fires his weapon the situation is critical; he shoots as a last resort. That wasn't the case here, but I refused to let that VC move into my company headquarters. I picked up my M-16, flipped the selector to full automatic, and aimed.

The black-clad soldier presented a tough target, dodging and ducking while the M-60 peppered the ground around him. He didn't realize I stood on the mound, watching his approach. Finally, deciding the M-60 gunner couldn't hit him, I squeezed the trigger. The burst caught the VC full in the chest, and he died as he crumpled to the ground.

"One, this is Six. Cease firing. One Victor Charlie Kilo India Alpha," I radioed, notifying the patrol that the Viet Cong was KIA. The bullets stopped raining down from the hill.

I asked my medic and a couple of riflemen to accompany me, and we snaked through the tall grass until we reached the VC's body. I smelled sour rice and sweat and blood as I bent over him. His weapon, an American M-16 rifle, lay beside his right hand. I wondered about the fate of the former owner.

We didn't find papers or identification of any kind on the dead man. Two loaded M-16 magazines, taped together, protruded from the rifle, but he carried no grenades or extra ammunition. He possessed only the weapon, his boots, and the bloody and torn black pajamas that clothed his limp form. The riflemen dug a shallow grave, and we buried the enemy soldier.

Back at my command post in the little saddle between the knolls, overlooking the Viet Cong's grave, I told my RTO to report the enemy contact to battalion headquarters. I sat down to review the recent action.

If I had killed the deer, the VC would have heard the shot, and probably lived. He quite likely belonged to the 48th VC Battalion, a unit we had battled for months. Perhaps his military specialty called for him to set booby traps along trails and plant land mines in hedgerow openings. My troops encountered booby traps and land mines all too frequently.

Should I have attempted to capture him? Past experience said no. Too many times we sent VC suspects to the rear, where interrogators released them to fight again. Furthermore, any capture attempt could have resulted in injuries to my men. Even though the enemy soldier didn't have much chance against the machine gun and my rifle, neither did my men have much chance against the insidious booby traps, an invisible menace that frustrated the hell out of us and killed or maimed many fine men.

I got paid to make decisions. I decided not to kill the deer. I decided to kill the Viet Cong soldier. I wonder why I can't decide, after all these years, to put the incident out of my mind.

Chapter 20

Holiday Swamp

Infantry companies operated as separate platoons, which at night were divided into squads that conducted ambushes. That was the 198th Infantry Brigade's policy in 1970–1971 in Vietnam. The idea was to saturate the countryside and keep the enemy away from populated areas. Each evening, companies transmitted to battalion headquarters the night defensive position of each element of the scattered unit. Woe unto the company that reported a single location, indicating that the unit occupied one NDP.

As Thanksgiving Day, 1970, approached, Charlie Company patrolled between the Tra Bong road and LZ Stinson. We moved continually, struggling under heavy packs, cursing the rains, and suffering from skin ulcers that developed from constant immersion.

As the commander, I declared the holiday a day of rest so my troops could dry out and enjoy a hot meal. The Thanksgiving Day meal would arrive by helicopter, and logic implied that, with each company widely dispersed, some men wouldn't receive hot meals. To hell with policy; on Thanksgiving Eve I assembled my entire company in a pacified village. The location was easy to defend, and having everybody in one place would simplify meal delivery.

When I transmitted Charlie Company's night location to LZ Stinson all hell broke loose. Apparently the entire war effort was in jeopardy because my soldiers gathered together for Thanksgiving.

After the battalion commander finished screaming over the radio, he finally realized the futility of ordering my company to disperse. Moving in the rain-obscured darkness without prior reconnaissance just wasn't smart. He grumbled some more, then signed off.

The rain stopped by the following morning, and hot food arrived in mid-afternoon. The aroma of roast turkey and mashed potatoes arose from the insulated containers when we opened them. The troops not guarding the perimeter lined up about five meters apart and shuffled forward, one at a time, to fill their mess kits with the holiday meal. Then they rested, read letters from home, wrote letters, and dried their sore feet.

While I was eating my mashed potatoes, turkey, stuffing and cranberry sauce, all mixed together on a metal tray and washed

Thanksgiving meal arrives near Nhan Hoa.
November 1970

down with Kool-Aid, the battalion commander called on the radio, ordering me to conduct a night raid on a ville located several kilometers to our east. Furthermore, we were to conduct the raid that night, on the Thanksgiving holiday. Additionally, we were to separate into platoons and remain separated. Disgruntled because I had allowed my troops to relax together for a few hours while we gave thanks for just being alive, he was retaliating.

I studied my map, determined the best route to the ville, and wondered how to avoid the mines and booby traps that I knew awaited us in the smothering darkness. Clouds marched overhead, and rain fell once more on Charlie Company. I briefed my platoon leaders and we prepared to move.

Dusk erased the daylight, and heavy rain drenched us. In almost total blackness, Charlie Company moved out onto the Tra Bong road. My artillery forward observer and I followed closely behind the point man, counting paces to record the distance traveled. In the complete darkness, we couldn't rely on terrain features to judge distance.

When the pace count reached the correct number, I informed the point man, and he led us south, away from the road. Now we followed a compass heading, a tough task because of the heavy rain, trees, bamboo thickets, and swamps.

A short distance from the road we entered a swamp, stumbling through chest-deep water and muck. Thoughts of snakes interfered with concentrating on the pace count, and the mud that sucked at our boots compounded the problem.

We eventually oozed up out of the swamp onto firm ground. After stumbling along for perhaps a kilometer, we halted, set up a defensive perimeter, and the troops dropped their rucks in preparation for the raid. The other platoons, now separated in the approved manner, called in their locations.

I briefed the leader of the raid and the raiders departed, leaving a small security force with the rucks and the company headquarters.

The security group also acted as a reaction force if the platoon required support.

When ready to begin the raid, although uncertain whether he was adjacent to the right ville, the platoon leader radioed his position to me. I called for artillery illumination. The troops charged into the collection of huts and searched the ville, awakening a few disgruntled women and children. The raid accomplished nothing, other than punishing the men of Charlie Company because their commander had violated a policy.

At daybreak we backtracked to the road, guided by our footprints in the mud. Near the road our tracks emerged from that miserable swamp. Everyone stopped, looked, and cursed.

The swamp measured one hundred yards wide, and our tracks emerged from the exact center of it. If we had turned off the road fifty yards sooner or fifty yards later, we would have avoided it completely. Navigating in the darkness, there had been no way to know the limits of the swamp.

I knew the limits of my men, however, and we marched until I found an easily defended area where we stopped, established security, and rested. Right then I named the quagmire Holiday Swamp.

The next Thanksgiving Day, those of us who survived were back in "the world," safe and dry. We didn't have to conduct pointless night raids after consuming the turkey. We didn't have to divide our families into small groups either.

Chapter 21

Mines and Booby Traps

Mines and booby traps awaited us on trails and in abandoned hooches, and enemy snipers lurked in jungles and in occupied villes. We often encountered mines and snipers in the same area, particularly near and in Dodge City. There wasn't much I could do about the mines, but I decided to change my tactics when conducting air assaults near villes, hoping to avoid the sniper fire we frequently encountered when we landed in open rice paddies.

On our next combat air assault into Dodge City, I directed the choppers to insert us practically on top of the huts. The tactic worked, and the assault went well. We occupied a cluster of hooches without taking fire.

Reacting to an intelligence report of an enemy position on a nearby hill, I instructed a platoon leader to dispatch a patrol. Intelligence reports were usually old when I got them, the enemy gone before we arrived. Not this time.

An explosion ripped the hill, filling me with dread. Because I hadn't cleared artillery fire into that area, I feared the patrol had hit a mine. I was wrong. The patrol radioed that the explosion occurred 200 meters to their front. They crept toward the hill, cautious and curious.

An hour later the patrol returned, carrying a wounded VC in a stretcher that the men had made from two bamboo poles and a pair of ponchos. In agony, bleeding freely, the VC had lost most of his private parts in the explosion. I told my medic to treat him, then called for a medevac chopper.

Our assault into the village had cut off the Viet Cong soldier's usual escape route. Surprised, he dashed along a different path, ran into a trip wire, and exploded his own mine. My troops rejoiced at that news.

My company field strength, seldom as high as 130 men, dropped to a low of 75 soldiers, with mines causing many of the losses. Most of the mines we encountered were made from our own ordnance, either captured by the enemy or purchased on the black market. The most common booby traps were hand grenades attached to trip wires strung across trails or openings in hedgerows. Others consisted of 81 mm mortar shells, 105 mm artillery rounds, and claymore mines. All had a devastating effect on mind and body.

Near Thach An Noi 3, one soldier tripped a wire attached to a 105 mm round, blowing him high into the air and blasting off both arms and both legs. His buddy, rushing to help the wounded man, hit a second mine, which killed the would-be rescuer. The first man survived, although I don't know how. Members of his platoon carried him from the hill in a poncho, blood sloshing around what was left of his body. Jagged ends of white bone were the only remnants of what had been his limbs. He remained conscious until we loaded him aboard the dust-off chopper. He asked me to hold his hand. I couldn't. He didn't have hands any more.

If we walked the rice paddies to avoid the trails, we were exposed to grazing fire away from cover. If we walked the trails to take advantage of cover and concealment, we ran into mines and booby traps. The VC attached electrical wire to mines and buried the explosive devices in well-used trails. The hidden wires ran to concealed enemy positions. The local Vietnamese walked the trails without danger; when we came along, a hidden VC detonated the buried mine by pressing the end of the wire against the terminals of a PRC-25 battery. Such mines were impossible to detect, their overlying dirt having been trod upon by countless feet.

In our night defensive positions, we remained alert for attempts by the VC to crawl to our claymores and turn them around. If they did, and if we fired our claymores in an ensuing attack, we blew ourselves away with our own weapons.

One of the enemy's favorite tricks was to mine our NDPs after we departed. If we returned to the location, we triggered trip wires or stumbled onto bouncing betty mines hidden in the grass. I made it policy never to reoccupy an NDP. However, other units operating in that area didn't know the locations of our former positions. Disaster awaited them if they ventured into old NDPs.

The loss of men to mines dealt a tremendous blow to our morale. We couldn't shoot back at an exploded mine, nor attack it with gunships or tactical air strikes. We could only pick up the pieces, literally, and continue on, searching for the elusive VC who knew the land intimately. We learned our area, knew where we could maneuver, then moved to a new area, and learned new lessons.

Finally we left, our tour complete, and our replacements learned their lessons the way we learned ours—one misstep at a time. After-action reports of lessons learned helped, but learning how to fight an elusive enemy by reading reports didn't replace experience. Nevertheless, I didn't want to remain in Vietnam to ensure that the lessons I learned were not forgotten. Two years was long enough.

On LZ Stinson, Chaplain James Masteller conducts a memorial service
for five Charlie Company soldiers killed in action.
December 1970

Chapter 22

Spider Hole

I heard shouts, followed by M-16 rifle fire. I gulped down my mouthful of C ration peaches, grabbed my rifle, and ran through the scattered trees toward the sounds of combat. Separated from us by a dry field, two men in black pajamas, one staggering, disappeared into a tree line.

"What's up?" I asked the point man.

"Two VC, Sir. They were in the field when we surprised 'em. I yelled, "*Lai day* (Come here)," but they wouldn't come. Instead, they took off, so I fired 'em up. Hit one pretty good too."

"OK, let's go find them." I told the platoon sergeant to lead a patrol to the distant tree line. When they reached the trees, the rest of us joined them.

Just inside the tree line, a mud-and-straw hut divided a grove of bamboo. Two women sat cross-legged on the dirt floor, weaving grass baskets and attempting to appear nonchalant. I asked them where the two men went, and they responded they didn't know what I was talking about. The Viet Cong held this village in a stranglehold, and I seldom gained any worthwhile information from talking to inhabitants here in Booby Trap Alley.

The platoon sergeant raised his voice. "Hey, CO, I've got a blood trail over here."

I walked around the bamboo thicket and saw the fresh blood smeared on a tree trunk. At the tree's base, the faint outline of a two-foot-square crack in the soil, half covered by leaves and grass, suggested an enemy spider hole.

The platoon sergeant, scared but determined, cut a bamboo pole and began prying at the crack. A square cover, beveled so it settled perfectly into a wooden frame embedded in the ground, loosened enough to allow the sergeant to insert the pole underneath.

"Hold it, Sarge," I said. "Let me talk them out, if I can."

In Vietnamese, I told them to surrender or they would die in the hole. The enemy didn't respond. We couldn't tell if the entrance led to a simple spider hole or a tunnel complex. Time to find out.

The sergeant handed the pole to another soldier, pulled the pin on a grenade, nodded, and, when the man raised the cover, tossed the grenade into the hole.

An instant after the muffled explosion, the sergeant poked the muzzle of his M-16 into the hole and sprayed an entire magazine into the underground hiding place. Quiet returned to the hamlet.

After the smoke cleared, the sergeant wormed into the hole, peering into the darkness. Two minutes later he surfaced, dragging a body with him.

"It's a long spider hole, CO. The other VC is dead, too." He muscled both bodies to the surface, then searched the burrow for weapons. He found two hand grenades, but nothing else.

Now the women reacted, wailing and calling us names, wringing their hands and sobbing. Tears streamed down their wrinkled faces, splashing into the dust. Were the dead men husbands, boyfriends, relatives, or acquaintances? I didn't know. Nor did I care.

The hole could provide concealment for other VC, so I requested explosives from our firebase. Within the hour a chopper landed in the dry field, and the door gunner handed out a 40-pound shaped charge. We moved the women away from the hut, then hunkered down nearby. The sergeant placed the charge in the hole and lit the fuse.

Boom! Dirt and bamboo soared into the air, then thumped down around us. The adjacent hut collapsed. The women screamed some more, then disappeared down a trail, probably to set fresh booby traps.

We had reduced the VC population in Booby Trap Alley by two. Their deaths didn't compensate for the twelve men I had lost in that area, but those two would set no more booby traps.

I opened another can of C rations and finished my lunch. I washed it down with swigs of warm water from my canteen, glancing occasionally at the flies crawling on the shattered enemy bodies.

Chapter 23

A Booby-Trapped Landing Zone

M icro-management started in the White House and trickled through layers of bureaucrats, diplomats, and senior military leaders. While the Vietnam War was still in its infancy, the concept of micro-management permeated the lower levels, infecting infantry companies and platoons. Why, when careers hung in the balance, should a leader risk letting a subordinate use his own initiative, make his own decisions?

Why? Because the leader on the ground usually had a better grasp of the immediate situation than battalion and brigade commanders and their staff officers who orbited in their command-and-control helicopters high above the battlefield. I'll cite a tragic example.

Charlie Company lifted from LZ Stinson in helicopters, en route to multiple landing zones that I had selected carefully based on my knowledge of the objective. I had been there before and knew the locations of previously occupied NDPs that—for safety's sake—must be avoided.

Confident in my selection of LZs, I relaxed en route, hoping that each platoon would find its LZ cold. When my helicopter flared prior to landing, I got ready to jump into the rice paddy that was to be the LZ for my company command group and the first platoon. Instead, I landed on dry ground that rose above the paddy. I looked around the two-ship LZ, realized we were in the middle of an old NDP, and turned to warn the platoon leader, who had landed in the chopper behind me.

BOOM! Shrapnel whizzed past me like a swarm of angry bees.

When the point man from the second chopper ran through a hedgerow opening, he hit an enemy trip wire, detonating the attached 81 mm mortar shell. The explosion killed two men outright and seriously wounded three others, including the platoon leader.

I called my departing helicopter pilot and requested that he return to extract the dead and wounded. We loaded them on board, and then I told my men to follow me as I cautiously moved through the thick hedge and off the LZ. With trembling legs and a dry mouth, I looked for wires or disturbed earth in the hedgerow, which would warn me of mines. I encountered nothing, and we escaped further casualties.

The battalion commander and his operations officer orbited overhead. I called on the radio, expressing my rage at being inserted into one of my old NDPs. I asked why we had been diverted, and why I hadn't been informed of the change.

The operations officer told me that he made the change so we wouldn't get our feet wet landing in the adjacent rice paddy. He made the decision at the last moment, and he said he didn't have time to inform me.

When I replied that I wouldn't have knowingly landed in that old position under any conditions, the battalion commander's voice came screaming from the radio, informing me that he wouldn't have any element leader of his showing remorse for casualties suffered in combat. He continued screaming, but I ignored him and turned off my radio as we consolidated our security. The remaining choppers hovered above the rice paddy, depositing my men safely into water up to their knees.

Both the operations officer and the battalion commander had commanded infantry companies, and I expect that they did a good job. However, now that they occupied positions of higher authority, they succumbed to the urge to micro-manage subordinate units, including mine.

The senseless casualties that resulted when a staff officer diverted us from the proper LZ have haunted me all of these years. Was I also guilty of micro-managing? I'd like to think that I wasn't, but some of my platoon leaders might have a different opinion.

There is a fine line between providing leadership and guidance, and over-managing. During the Vietnam era, in some units, leaders crossed that line. It's no wonder such a condition evolved, considering the example set by the White House and Department of Defense.

Chapter 24

Jungle Scars

During lulls in combat, I often looked across the bright green rice paddies of Vietnam to the Annamite Mountains shimmering in the heat waves. Surrounded by beauty yet exposed to the ugliness of war, I yearned to view the scenery unfiltered by the heat and mud of the battlefields.

I begged a plane ride with an Air Force FAC (forward air controller). The FAC had told me about a planned bombing mission in the mountains to the west, and I took advantage of the opportunity to see that jungle-covered terrain from the air. I knew all too well what it looked like from ground level.

We flew in an OV-10 Bronco—a twin-engine, two-place spotter plane—with the mission of marking an NVA base camp with white phosphorous rockets, thus enabling an Australian bomber crew, flying a Canberra, to identify the target.

Flying over the jungle that clung to the nearly vertical sides of the mountains, I doubted that the enemy would build a base camp in such terrain. It seemed a shame to blast apart the beautiful green canopy that, from our altitude, resembled sponges on the bottom of a clear lagoon.

Fred, the pilot, dived the plane toward the location that military intelligence identified as a base camp, jinking to avoid any ground fire. Near the bottom of the dive he fired a rocket into the triple-canopy jungle, which promptly swallowed the smoke. The plane immediately shot upward at maximum rate-of-climb, as green tracers zipped past the plane's cockpit. Right then I changed my mind about blasting the jungle.

On our next dive to launch another rocket, tracers from several weapons seemed to float up at us. They missed. Fred fired his second rocket, hauling back on the control yoke as the plane clawed for altitude, corkscrewing to avoid the enemy fire.

We circled while Fred directed the Australian bomber crew into the target area. A hint of smoke rose through the tree canopy below, and the bomber made its run, dropping the first bomb close to the marker.

Fred radioed adjustments to the bomber pilot, and the Aussies dropped three more bombs, deadly accurate. Our low pass to assess damage, free from ground fire this time, revealed massive destruction of the base camp, at least the portion above ground. It would have been an ideal time for our infantry to move in and mop up, but the nearest infantry unit was miles away, otherwise engaged.

For this infantryman, aerial combat presented an intense, yet detached, experience. It seemed impersonal, remote. When receiving ground fire, which I couldn't hear, the passion of intense combat—such as when I engaged the enemy in the jungle or across a rice paddy—didn't exist. I did feel vulnerable and longed to dig in or find a tree or dike to use for cover. There are no paddy dikes to hide behind 500 feet in the air.

The mission complete, we turned toward Chu Lai and a shower and hot meal, a luxury denied an infantryman after a ground battle. En route, I asked Fred to perform a few aerobatics, and he gladly obliged. High over the jungle, Fred snapped the plane into a series of barrel rolls, chandelles and an Immelmann turn, concluding with a loop.

I loved it, smiling at the incongruous situation. When combat ended on the ground, I dealt with many demands, such as consolidation, resupply, attending to any wounded, and preparing for counterattacks. Now, after an air combat mission, I cartwheeled across the sky as if celebrating the end of the war. The stark differences between aerial and ground combat made me question my decision to be an infantryman.

Why did I volunteer to fly as a passenger on a combat mission? In addition to viewing the country's beauty from above, I wanted a different perspective of the war. As an infantryman, my view suffered from limitations imposed by the enemy sniping from hedgerows, or automatic weapons blasting from clumps of bamboo across rice paddies. My view from helicopters was restricted by the knowledge that in minutes we would be assaulting another LZ, with good odds it would be adjacent to an enemy position. One doesn't enjoy the view under such conditions, nor give any thought to environmental damage.

I looked back at the mountain after completing the bombing mission. The white-brown scar we had created was clearly visible midst the emerald jungle.

The evidence of our air strike likely disappeared within a few years. Other scars of that war, although invisible, remain.

Chapter 25

A Christmas Birth

The clink, clink of an entrenching tool against dirt and stones, the rustle of jungle fatigues, and the soldiers' whispers disturbed the quiet evening as we developed our NDP in the waning minutes of daylight. I inspected the fighting positions, checking fields of fire, claymore mines, and overall security.

We occupied an area new to us, away from Dodge City, away from that breeding ground of booby traps and mines and endless sniping. We had spent the afternoon humping our rucks toward LZ Stinson, still some five kilometers away, where we would replace one of our sister companies for three days, providing security for the firebase and eating hot meals instead of the tasteless combat rations.

Higher headquarters had announced a temporary cease-fire starting at 1800 the next day: Christmas Eve, 1970. We wouldn't slog onto Stinson until Christmas afternoon, thus assuring that both my company and the one that we would replace would have an opportunity to eat a hot holiday meal. Meanwhile, we prepared for another night in the Nam.

We arranged our NDP in an irregular circle around a farmer's mud-and-bamboo hut. A short distance from the dwelling a barn of similar construction, but open on one side, sheltered a cow. Hay, stacked in one end of the tiny barn, provided food for the dun-colored animal. Her slender neck and legs accentuated her swollen sides. She munched her hay while keeping a wary eye on the nearby foreigners.

I dug a position between the barn and the hut, where I could direct the action if the enemy probed our defenses during the night.

Around midnight, a low moan woke me. I listened—alert, cautious, assessing. The faint groans continued sporadically, seeming to come from the barn. I rose, walked in the faint moonlight to the barn, and saw a newborn calf lying on the dirt floor while its mother licked its wet coat. The cow rolled her eyes at me, flared her nostrils, then continued cleaning her calf.

After checking a few defensive positions I lay down again, smiling at the timing of the calf's birth. Amid the horrors of war, the miracle of birth, especially at Christmastime, calmed me. For a brief interlude I looked at life, rather than death.

The troops delighted in looking at the calf the next day, before we struggled into our packs and continued the march toward LZ Stinson. Near the base of the hill that buttressed the firebase, we stopped and again set up an NDP. The cease-fire was in effect. It was Christmas Eve.

Cold rain fell, along with my spirits. Far from home and lonely, I thought of my family and our Christmas Eve traditions. My men, each with his own memories, hunkered under ponchos, as lonesome and miserable in the rain as I. Yet a commander is uniquely alone, unable to really share his feelings with his men.

In my pack, safely cushioned in a pair of socks, were two miniature bottles of Scotch. Those bottles had ridden safely in that pack since I assumed command of Charlie Company several months before. They would ride there no more.

I called for the platoon leader whose platoon I accompanied, and produced the tiny bottles. Sitting there in the rain and darkness, I toasted the newborn calf back in the tiny ville and drank to better times. The platoon leader joined me in the toast, surprised at the opportunity to enjoy a Christmas drink under such circumstances.

We discussed hunting, of all things, whispering just loud enough to be heard above the rain that sounded like hurled gravel as it spattered onto our ponchos. We swapped yarns for a couple of hours. The two ounces of Scotch disappeared long before we ran out of hunting stories.

Chapter 26

Christmas Day, 1970

On Christmas afternoon, Charlie Company trooped onto LZ Stinson, where we celebrated with a rare hot meal. The cooks worked hard to present us with roast turkey, dressing, and most of the traditional dishes that make up Americans' Christmas dinner. We even had fresh cookies and apple pie.

The battalion chaplain conducted a religious service, and I silently thanked God for His guidance and prayed for the courage to again lead my company after the cease-fire ended.

The rain stopped and we dried our feet and clothing, thinking ahead to the next mission, just two days away. Christmas would be a memory, and so would the cease fire.

Late on Christmas Day, my RTO sat on the ground, opening a package from home that contained Christmas decorations and gifts. He held up a small cardboard angel, a red corrugated-paper bell, and a miniature Christmas stocking filled with hard candy and assorted trinkets. Reminders of a holiday best spent with family surrounded him as he spread the gifts on the ground. He grinned, but the grin lacked conviction, revealing instead suppressed emotion—loneliness that Christmas gifts couldn't overcome. While he sat inside his circle of ornaments, I snapped a photo and then turned away, leaving space for us both. We wrapped ourselves in memories, forgetting the dragons and monsters for a little while.

Our artillery was silent. Accustomed to the intermittent explosions of H&I fire whenever we guarded the firebase, the silence unsettled us. Would the enemy take advantage of the cease-fire and infiltrate our perimeter? Would the VC place mines on the trails that we would trudge down when we left the hill on our next mission?

Even if the VC played by the rules of the cease-fire, their booby traps and mines lay in endless ambush.

When the sun went down, I laced up my boots and strolled around the perimeter, sharing a Christmas greeting with my soldiers, who rested inside bunkers. I ignored the odor of marijuana. Word of my route along the defensive positions preceded me, and no one smoked pot when I was around. Guards sat atop the bunkers, staring into the night, watching for movement and listening for unusual noises. Someone turned on a radio or tape player, and the faint sound of "Winter Wonderland" filtered through the bunker's firing port.

At the other end of the firebase, a generator throbbed and rattled as it produced electricity to power tactical radios and electric lights. Guards standing near the generator relied solely on their eyes during their two-hour tour of duty.

I had to check for messages, so I climbed the knoll to reach my command bunker where my RTOs took turns manning the company radios. A rat scurried across the path and disappeared.

Christmas Day. Merry Christmas. Bah, humbug.

Captain Lee Basnar on Hill 85 near LZ Stinson.
Christmas Day 1970

Chapter 27

Change of Command

I had commanded Charlie Company for six months in this, my second tour. I began to wonder if I could possibly survive this war, if I could live until my DEROS. I was an infantry commander, hardened and honed on the grindstone of combat, but I was also human, and I was tired. How much longer could I effectively command? Would weariness dull my edge and endanger my soldiers? Doubt began to infiltrate my confidence.

I received word that my duties in the field would end after the next mission. The 198th Infantry Brigade commander had selected me to be his Assistant Brigade Operations Officer in charge of the brigade Tactical Operations Center (TOC) in Chu Lai. My senior platoon leader, scheduled for promotion to captain within a couple of weeks, would replace me as company commander.

My conscience collided with my sense of self-preservation as the remaining time with my company grew short. We had fought many battles beside one another, my men and I, and they had responded well to my demands. Was it fair that I was to be assigned to a job in the rear when they had to remain in the field? I rationalized my transfer, knowing that most company commanders served in the position for a maximum of six months. The constant stress and pressure of command wore us down. Our wounded and dead soldiers became our personal failures, loading us with guilt. A new commander would bring fresh leadership to Charlie Company.

The day before I was scheduled to transfer my command, my RTO motioned to me to answer a radio call. A platoon RTO requested a dust-off for a wounded soldier. The officer who was to replace me led that platoon. I called for the dust-off and then asked for a spot report on the action. The platoon sergeant told me over the radio that a bullet had struck my replacement's arm; the extent of his injuries was unknown. I had lost another platoon leader, and I didn't know what the future now held for me. I didn't sleep much that night, as usual.

A week later, a chopper deposited the wounded platoon leader at my field location, unannounced, and he flashed a big grin as he jumped from the Huey. He told me that while he directed action in a firefight, a bullet tore through the fleshy part of the underside of his arm, halfway between his elbow and shoulder. The AK-47 round went in one side and exited the other, drilling a neat little hole but missing the bone. He showed me the Band-Aids that covered the entrance and exit holes, and said he felt fine and was ready to assume command of Charlie Company.

Unable to muster appropriate words as the toughest, most rewarding job of my life drew to a close, I gave the new company commander my map, my wristwatch, and my best wishes. With the helicopter waiting, I had no time to say good-bye to my men, other than to the few soldiers in my immediate vicinity.

I climbed aboard the chopper, right arm raised in a final salute to the men of Charlie Company. The chopper gained altitude, and the finest soldiers I ever led grew small and disappeared. My eyes filled with tears. Guilt rode on my shoulders, heavier than my combat pack. Why had I been allowed to survive, unwounded, while others around me were shattered or killed?

I turned to look ahead, peering between the aircraft commander and the copilot. Through the chopper's windscreen I saw a distant sparkle on the far horizon. I looked toward the months I had left to serve in country, grateful to be alive.

As I left the dark jungles and flooded rice paddies behind, the waters of the South China Sea appeared ahead, shimmering in the sun, the waves rolling in from across vast distances. Somewhere beyond the sea lay my country, a land where my loved ones waited, and to which I was eager to return. I had spent a total of eighteen months in this country, and had to remain for six more.

The war continued.

Part III

On the Way. Wait.

Chapter 29

Surrounded

The radio crackled, breaking squelch. A faint whisper hissed over the receiver's hum.

"Hammer Three Alpha, this is Recon Six, do not transmit. Over." Alerted, I listened intently to the urgent whisper of the LRRP team leader. The Long-Range Reconnaissance Patrol, working in the mountainous jungle west of Chu Lai, didn't initiate radio calls unless in imminent danger. Under normal conditions the unit maintained radio listening silence, breaking squelch twice at prescribed intervals to let the Tactical Operations Center know they still lived. In charge of the TOC, I listened, not answering. Within minutes the LRRP team leader radioed again, still whispering.

"Hammer Three Alpha, this is Recon Six. I say again, do not transmit. We have movement in several places outside our perimeter. Be prepared to extract us on call. If you roger, break squelch twice. Over."

I nodded to my RTO, who depressed the transmit button twice, answering the LRRP team.

LRRP teams conducted reconnaissance in small groups, which normally consisted of a team leader, a medic, an RTO, and four or five other men. Their missions varied, but usually the recon teams provided information about enemy movement. During periods of low lunar illumination, the teams patrolled an area we called the Rocket Pocket, named for a jungled collection of peaks and valleys where the enemy launched 122 mm rockets aimed at the Americal Division Combat Base. If the LRRPs detected the enemy setting up rocket launchers, we pounded the launch sites using artillery, helicopter gunships, or tactical air strikes.

This LRRP team hid in the Rocket Pocket now. The sound of movement near their perimeter, and from more than one location, forewarned of their being surrounded and annihilated.

I alerted an artillery unit to stand by for a fire mission, and then returned to the radio.

Within ten minutes the team leader whispered again.

"Hammer Three Alpha, this is Recon Six. We now have movement progressing around our left flank. I estimate a platoon-size enemy force is moving into position around us. Stand by and do not transmit. Out."

I alerted an extraction team, consisting of two lift helicopters and two helicopter gunships, telling them to be prepared for immediate launch. They well understood the difficulty of a night extraction in dense jungle, particularly under intense enemy fire.

Time crawled toward daylight, increasing the chances of a successful extraction. No one spoke in the tension-filled TOC. An RTO popped open a Coke can, startling the rest of us.

"Hammer Three Alpha, this is Recon Six. We now have movement to our south. We're going to blow our claymores and open fire. Stand by. Out."

Another ten minutes dragged by. Was the LRRP team heavily engaged with the enemy? Could we rescue them if they requested extraction? Any casualties? A strong voice came over the radio, not the quiet whisper of previous transmissions.

"Hammer Three Alpha, this is Recon Six. Over."

I answered the call. "Recon Six, this is Hammer Three Alpha. Over."

"This is Recon Six. We blew our claymores and fired up the area. We received negative incoming fire. Have heard negative further movement. We'll remain in place until daylight, then conduct a search. Request extraction one hour after daybreak. Over."

"This is Hammer Three Alpha. Wilco on the extraction. Out."

About half an hour after daybreak we heard from the team one final time.

"Hammer Three Alpha, this is Recon Six. Over."

"Recon Six, this is Hammer Three Alpha. Over."

"This is Recon Six. Spot report follows. Initiated contact with a suspected platoon-size enemy force after hearing movement completely around our perimeter. Fired claymores and small arms. Received negative incoming fire. Swept the contact area at first light. Results: one Victor Charlie black bear Kilo India Alpha. Negative friendly casualties. End of spot report. We're ready for extraction. Out."

A wandering black bear had circled the small group of men in the darkness, convincing the patrol that the enemy surrounded them. The LRRP's weapons killed the bear.

In the TOC we added a new category to our kill list:

VC Black Bears KIA: One.

Chapter 30

Luck

Roaring through the night, an enemy 122 mm rocket smashed into a hooch across the dusty street from mine, and I rolled from my cot onto the floor. Sandbags that surrounded my hooch in the 198th Infantry Brigade headquarters area protected me from whizzing shrapnel. I lay there, tense, wondering where the next rocket would land. The enemy launched the rockets from the Rocket Pocket, a jungle-covered collection of mountains to our west. The VC targeted the airfield and ammunition dumps, but the inaccurate rockets often fell short or landed long. This one landed long.

I rose and ran across the street. The rocket had exploded on impact with the hooch, killing a soldier with one day remaining in Vietnam. Medics removed his body, but much of his blood remained, staining a piece of the shattered plywood wall. I thought again about my astounding luck. I recalled my first tour, when a mortar round exploded in the hooch next to mine, similar to this incident. That time another soldier shared my luck, for he was on R&R in Hawaii when the explosion shattered his bunk.

I recalled an evening in the High Ground when one of my platoon leaders and I talked quietly just before dark. A burst of bullets from an AK-47 sliced the air between us, missing us both.

I thought of the many other times the bullets and the shrapnel missed me, and of the men who weren't so lucky. Luck is fickle; I prayed she would remain with me until my tour ended in just a few more days.

Chapter 31

Last Chopper Ride

With only three days left in country, I wasn't short; I was next. I could now count hours, instead of days, until I would rejoin my wife and daughter. Then the brigade commander told me to visit several firebases on a mission that has been flushed from my memory. Perhaps I had to distribute some secret message or new communications codes. I wasn't eager to fly over enemy-occupied terrain again with so little time left before my DEROS, and I took extra ammo for my M-16 in case we made an unplanned landing in some remote location away from friendly troops.

I climbed into the helicopter on the landing pad adjacent to brigade headquarters and gave the pilot directions. We visited several hilltop firebases and observation posts, each one susceptible to enemy fire at any moment. We touched down at one after the other without incident until there remained just one more base to visit.

En route to Hill 411, an observation post perched on a hill that rose 411 meters above sea level, turbulence slammed into the chopper. We dropped a hundred feet in a couple of seconds, and I grabbed for any handhold I could reach, certain that my luck had finally run out. The enemy hadn't killed me, but the turbulence threatened to.

The pilot regained control of the LOH-6 chopper and grinned at me as I, with jaw clenched and muscles taut, gripped the aircraft seat. I was not amused.

Upon completion of my tasks we returned to Chu Lai, where I exhibited great self-control by refraining from kissing the ground. The pilot pantomimed checking for brown stains on the seat I had occupied. I saluted him with one finger.

Chapter 32

The Freedom Bird

T he Day finally arrived. I suffered the wrath of grapes from par-
tying with my fellow officers the night before. Traditionally, a
departing officer bought the booze while his peers toasted his success in surviving the war, and alcohol flowed freely. The sun added
to my misery by preheating the C-130 that I boarded for the trip to
Cam Ranh Bay.

The noisy four-engine transport lifted from the runway and
turned south along the coast, giving me my last look at Chu Lai.
Once again, the beauty of the country impressed me, but I thought
mostly of the gallant men who remained behind. They continued to
fight under the broiling sun, counting the days until they, too, could
leave this tropical hell.

At Cam Ranh Bay, a sergeant informed us that our chartered
commercial jet had been delayed in Japan; our departure time remained uncertain. I spent nearly two days sweating in the breathless
heat, watching the hands on my watch creep around the dial. I
passed the time by reading or occasionally chatting with another

captain, the same one who still remembered the sapper-under-the-hooch guy from when we first arrived in country. We played cards and slowly sipped beer as the hours dragged on. We reminisced a little about the year that had just passed, but mostly we kept our thoughts to ourselves. We didn't want to talk about the war; we just wanted to go home.

Finally, shortly before midnight, the plane arrived and we boarded, smiling at the American female flight attendants as they welcomed us aboard the Freedom Bird. Their fragrant perfume reminded me of hot showers, soft mattresses, and home. The doors closed, the plane taxied into position for takeoff, and then the jet engines propelled us ever faster until we lifted from the runway. A great cheer erupted. We had finally left behind the odors, the noise, the heat, and the soil of Vietnam. We left behind a large portion of ourselves, too.

After that single outburst the soldiers grew quiet, withdrawing into themselves as they tried to cope with the memories of the year they had just experienced. It would forever remain in their minds, a year like no other in their lifetimes. Some would never adjust to civilian life. Others would adjust, but the memories of that year would emerge at unexpected times, usually at night.

I knew I wouldn't return to the country that rapidly disappeared into the night behind us. Two tours. Two years. Too much.

I never again faced combat, and I'm still amazed that I came through unscathed. There are, however, invisible scars. Sometimes I shake my memory duffel bag too hard, and long-buried images emerge. Dreams and infrequent nightmares crawl out of that duffel bag, and burying them again is sometimes difficult.

And I'm one of the lucky ones.

Epilogue

My men fought well. In any infantry company, there are soldiers who do just enough to get by and soldiers who do their job well but don't stand out in the crowd. Those men are, unfortunately, forgotten within a few years.

The soldiers who made the extra effort, volunteered for the toughest missions, walked point, and led their comrades when survival seemed doubtful—those are the troops I remember. They will remain in my memory forever as examples of true warriors, willing to risk their lives for their comrades. They had nicknames like Doc Holliday, Ranger, Baby Ranger, Spider, Canada, and many others. When I look at fading photos of those men, I recall the hardships we faced together and the bravery under fire.

My officers' performance ranged from excellent to outstanding. I relieved a couple of platoon leaders, sending them to jobs in the rear. One was incompetent, and I simply couldn't spend all of my time with his platoon trying to teach him how to lead. The other just wasn't cut out to be an infantry officer. He meant well, but just didn't have the gravel in his guts to be an infantryman. I wanted my soldiers to be led by the best officers available. Rather than leave weak officers in a leadership position, I replaced them with seasoned NCOs, at least until new lieutenants joined the company.

My first sergeant was one of the finest NCOs I ever served with. Top, as we called him, set the example for every soldier in Charlie Company. Much of the company's success was a direct result of his support. My executive officer was superb, as were most of those who led the platoons in Charlie Company. I was blessed with officers and noncommissioned officers whom I would follow anywhere.

The war deeply divided our nation. Despite the news of antiwar protests back home and the miserable conditions under which we struggled, American soldiers fought valiantly. Troops in my company on the battlefields of Vietnam seldom talked about patriotism or defending the South Vietnamese from their northern neighbors. No one mentioned making the world safe for democracy, or ensuring freedom of choice for the embattled people.

The men I served with fought for different reasons. They fought to protect their buddies. They fought because otherwise their peers might accuse them of cowardice. They fought because their leaders did, and they followed their leaders. A few fought for the medals they could wear with pride if they made it back to The World. Most men simply fought to stay alive.

Why did an infantryman, already at extreme risk, volunteer to be a point man, leading the way against unseen snipers or hidden mines and booby traps? Was it because he wanted to fight for democracy and freedom? No, he did it for a variety of reasons, but patriotism wasn't high on his list.

He became a point man because he was the best in his platoon at the dangerous chore. He took the point because he felt invincible, that his time on earth had not yet expired. He volunteered so his best friend wouldn't have to perform the risky job. He did it because he enjoyed being admired by his fellow infantrymen. He walked point because he had been there before, was an old hand in the unit, and could teach new men how to survive. A few point men became killers, thriving on the danger and the thrill of deadly combat. These men, in the minority, often became too bold and went home in body bags. Combat soldiers often paired up with a buddy, each pledging to look out for the other. One walked point while his buddy walked slack. The point man looked for trip wires and other signs of mines, and listened intently for suspicious sounds. The slack man looked farther ahead, beyond the point man, looking for snipers or other signs of the enemy. He also provided instant backup for the point man when they came under fire. The trust between these two individuals was complete, a bonding that would baffle rear-area soldiers.

I can't speak about the other services, or even for other infantry companies. Each unit developed its own personality, shaped by the skill of its leaders and its past successes and defeats. Charlie Company celebrated victories and suffered losses like any other unit, but even the losses forged the company's personality. My troops took a perverse pride in being assigned tough missions. They complained and fought on, proud to be infantrymen, honored to fulfill an important role in a good unit.

My soldiers seldom discussed patriotism, unless it was to speak with disdain of the cowards who fled the United States to avoid the draft. Survival was the name of the game. Locked in a contest in which, at our level, survival was the measure of victory, we left the discussion of patriotism, freedom, and democracy to politicians and senior military leaders. We discussed our fallen comrades, whether our M-16 rifle was as effective as the enemy's AK-47, and how many days we had left in country.

We would discuss patriotism when, and if, we returned home.

My return from each tour disheartened me. Some of my fellow citizens looked at me with disdain, called me a baby killer, spat upon me. Some hated the war and extended that hatred to the soldiers who fought in it.

I came home from my second tour in Vietnam determined never to return to that war. I planned to resign my commission and leave the army rather than accept another assignment to a war we were not permitted to win. I saw too many good men maimed and killed because of a flawed hierarchy that began with President Lyndon Johnson, extended through Secretary of Defense Robert McNamara, and invaded the upper levels of military leadership. Fortunately, the army didn't order me back to Vietnam. I completed my twenty years and retired.

In the spring of 1999, one of my platoon leaders and my executive officer joined me for three days at my home in Arizona. It was a reunion unlike any I had experienced up to that time. The mutual respect and admiration we still held for one another would baffle noncombatants. Although we hadn't seen one another for twenty-eight years, we still felt the strength of the bond. We always will. When we parted, we agreed to stay in touch.

Charlie Company's officers gathered in our nation's capital in the spring of 2001, marking our thirty-year reunion since we fought together in the stifling jungles and monsoon rains of Vietnam. Except for the two officers who had joined me in Arizona two years previously, I hadn't seen or heard from my leaders for thirty years. The emotion we felt upon seeing one another nearly overwhelmed us. Our families joined us, making our homecoming complete.

Thanks to superb planning by one of my former platoon leaders, that gathering of warriors was an event that will remain vivid in our minds until we draw our last breath. We attended the Evening Parade at the Marine Barracks at the invitation of President George W. Bush, laid a wreath at the Tomb of the Unknown Soldier, were invited for dinner at our former brigade commander's home, and were honored that our former division commander attended that remarkable evening with us. The commander of the artillery battalion that supported us in Vietnam was present, as well as our artillery forward observer. Our battalion chaplain and battalion surgeon joined us, and they spoke of Charlie Company's exploits with admiration and respect.

Our families learned a lot about us during our reunion, hearing perhaps for the first time the memories we had suppressed for three decades. We parted with renewed respect and admiration for one another, and a determination to start planning the next reunion. I regret that it's impossible to reunite with all of the soldiers who served with me in Charlie Company.

It is to the memory of the fighting officers and men of Charlie Company that I have written these stories of my service in the Vietnam War. When the final bugle blows taps and we meet again, the bond between us will still be there, rallying us around a different flag. Those who fell on the battlefields of Vietnam will welcome us as we, one at a time, join the eternal ranks of former Vietnam warriors.

Charlie Company warriors, I salute you all.

…Comrades-in-arms go marching by,
The living and the dead.
He reaches out to say goodbye —
They disappear instead…

Excerpt from the poem
"A Soldier Retires"
by Lee Basnar

Acknowledgments

One brief, but most important, tale of my experiences must be told. The tale began when I married Joan Chandler Basnar in 1956, and that story continues.

Joan, and our daughter, Lorraine, endured the long separations and the distress of watching the evening news, seeing graphic portrayals of what I was going through in Vietnam. My wife's calm, loving manner came through loud and clear in the many letters she wrote to me during my two years over there. Lorraine, too, sent me letters, and they both sent tapes of their voices at a time when affordable battery-operated portable tape decks were new. The emotion I felt the first time I played a tape and heard their voices was almost overwhelming.

I can't imagine serving in Vietnam without Joan's support, or returning to a home without her. She backed me wholeheartedly throughout my army career, and she continued that reinforcement while I wrote this book. Thank you, Joan—my childhood sweetheart, my wife, my best friend.

I'm grateful to our daughter, Lorraine Elder, for designing the book and the cover and for helping me understand how a computer works. Her help was invaluable, and her patience was remarkable.

Every writer needs an editor, and I'm grateful for the assistance that my editor, Kathy Bradley, provided in improving the organization of this book. Her attention to detail was outstanding, and she was a joy to work with.

About the Author

L ee Basnar's military career took him to Germany, France, Vietnam, Alaska, and several assignments in the continental United States. He rose through the enlisted ranks to Sergeant First Class E-7, received a direct commission, and retired as a Major. His enlisted duties included infantry squad leader and platoon sergeant, company first sergeant, and battalion operations sergeant. As an officer, he commanded a basic training company in South Carolina, an infantry company in Vietnam, and an area recruiting command in California, as well as serving in staff assignments as an inspector general, assistant secretary of the general staff, S-3 and G-3 operations officer, and advisor to the Alaska National Guard, among other duties.

After his retirement from the army in 1981, Lee and his wife, Joan, lived for sixteen years in the Alaska bush, where he ran a trapline; subsisted on fish and game; was a bush pilot; wrote articles for magazines, including *Alaska Magazine;* and operated a successful woodworking business. He also served on various Alaska and federal fish and game commissions, and as the bush representative to the U.S. Army Alaska Retiree Council.

The Basnars now live in Sierra Vista, Arizona, where Lee served as chairman of the city's Environmental Affairs Commission. He writes a regular column for the *Sierra Vista Herald* and maintains a keen interest in community affairs.

Dates of Service in Vietnam

June 1967–June 1968: Advisor to 22nd ARVN Infantry Division

September 1970–September 1971: Commander, C Company, 1st Battalion, 52nd Infantry; Assistant Operations Officer, 198th Infantry Brigade

Decorations

Distinguished Flying Cross

Bronze Star Medal with "V" and three oak leaf clusters

Meritorious Service Medal with oak leaf cluster

Air Medal, second award

Army Commendation Medal with oak leaf cluster

Good Conduct Medal, third award

National Defense Service Medal

Vietnam Service Medal with bronze star

Armed Forces Reserve Medal

Vietnamese Gallantry Cross with silver and bronze stars

Vietnamese Staff Service Honor Medal

Republic of Vietnam Campaign Medal

Order of Saint Maurice —with rank of Centurion

Combat Infantryman Badge

Printed in the United States
21472LVS00001B/418-501